BROOKE HAMLIN

Escaping Ordinary

Think Following Jesus Sounds Boring? Think Again

First edition

This book was professionally typeset on Reedsy.
Find out more at reedsy.com

To my dad, who wrote down his dreams for me on a piece of paper, then got on his knees and prayed over those words until they became a reality. Thanks for praying out me of ordinary.
I love you!

To my mom, the human sunshine, whose very presence in a room creates an extraordinary atmosphere. Thanks for making me write this book. I love you!

"It's high Christian adventure if your heart is in the right place. Because wherever you are, Jesus will be, too."

— Brother Andrew

Contents

Foreword

Writing this book felt a lot like matchmaking. I don't want to merely woo you with my words or entertain you with my stories.

I want to introduce you to Someone.

I've known Him for a while now, and I've got this gut feeling that He's the *One* for you. Plus, He's been dropping some not-so-subtle hints that He's interested in speaking with you. I hope these pages become your meeting place and that these words wriggle free, wrap their way around your heart, and place your hand in the waiting hand of Christ.

Then I'll watch with happy tears as you two ride away into the sunset, headed off on your very own adventures.

Maybe I'll even throw rice or something — blow some bubbles, light some sparklers, release some butterflies.

I know...**FIREWORKS!**

Definitely fireworks!

No matter what, it's gonna be a party!

I'll see you on the other side of ordinary.

1

My Accidental Modeling Career

My time had come. I could feel it in my bones. I was gonna *get famous!*

After years of poking and prodding from friends and family, I finally decided to audition for a singing competition television show. For weeks, I agonized over my song choice and dutifully practiced my best singing face in front of the mirror.

My mother graciously volunteered to tag along as my moral support. I repaid her generosity by belting out vocal exercises for two solid hours on the way to the nearest audition site.

I remember the shaky, sweet feeling of excitement as we exited the car and began wandering around the maze-like college campus where the auditions were being held. I smiled broadly at anyone we passed just in case they were someone important.

Couldn't hurt, I figured.

When we finally located the mobile studio —a giant RV plastered with fountain drink advertisements —I rolled back my shoulders, took a deep breath, and tried to look confident.

A nice-looking young girl was hanging out near the front of the studio, and I greeted her with my smiling and waving routine.

She smiled and returned the wave, seemingly relieved to find someone to talk to. "Where are you from?" she asked. After exchanging the basic introductory banter, she surprised me by instructing, "Now Rick's gonna wanna know you're here, so go introduce yourself, and he'll tell you what to do."

Rick, who was Rick? I tried not to let my smile falter under the weight of my confusion.

"Ok...where can I find him?" I fumbled.

"The director, Rick, he's back with the crew," she explained, "Just ask around until you find him!"

I thanked her and walked away, pretending like I knew exactly what was going on. It seemed strange to have all the contestants personally check in with the director, but I had never done anything like this before.

As I rounded the front of the studio, I was greeted by a handful of people, all obviously here to audition. A giant of a man, dressed in an all-white tuxedo and matching fedora, was leaning over a picnic table and singing to himself. None of these would-be superstars seemed to be mingling with the crew, and I felt increasingly certain the girl had made a mistake.

After some encouragement from my mother, however, I cautiously approached the flurry of activity near the front of the mobile studio. A cluster of men, dressed in black, bustled hurriedly about with clipboards and AV equipment.

I cleared my throat and tried to act like I belonged, "I'm looking for Rick?"

A tall man sporting an important-looking headset turned and walked towards me. "I'm supposed to tell you that I'm here," I offered weakly.

He reached out and took my hand, "I'm Rich."

My cheeks flushed with embarrassment. *Great, I called him the wrong name.*

Luckily, he didn't seem to notice my mistake and continued with growing enthusiasm, "I'm so glad you're here! I'll show you your outfit!"

I froze.

My outfit? What was going on here!?!

Not wanting to look uncooperative, I nodded numbly and followed him around the back of the van to a collection of blue, plastic tubs.

"Now, all you need to do is look through and find one of each that's in your size," he instructed, pointing out the contents of the various containers. "We used to have more accessories, but they've gotten lost along the way. Just make sure you get a shirt, pants, and shoes."

"Great!" I gave him my best enthusiastic grin and nodded like I understood precisely what he was saying.

"Oh, and you can either change in the van or the restrooms inside. It's a little cramped in the van, though," he explained.

"I'll change inside," I answered quickly, terrified at the prospect of trying to change near the horde of male crew members.

I waited until Rich had walked away before rifling through the tubs for myself. The first contained blue t-shirts emblazoned with a popular soft drink logo, the next contained white skinny jeans, another contained shoes, and a final tub contained various accessories like belts and sunglasses.

What was going on here!? My mind reeled with the possibilities.

3

Maybe they assigned an outfit to everyone who auditioned? Maybe it leveled the playing field or something? But if so, why didn't they mention anything about this on the website!? I had worked so hard picking out the clothes I had on. I was disappointed to have to change.

I held up a pair of skinny jeans and peered around the front of the van to take a second look at giant tuxedo man.

Yeah, there was no way he was fitting in these pants. Maybe they're only for the women?

I shrugged off my doubts and carefully selected one of each item. If they want me to wear this little blue outfit, I decided I would wear it like no one has ever worn it before!

I walked determinedly into the building and discovered the nice girl from earlier already in the bathroom. She had changed into an outfit just like mine and was preening herself in front of the mirror. "Don't worry," she said as I walked in, "They said it's gonna be super chill. All we have to do is pass out the soda."

Wait...what!? Pass out the soda!? What is she TALKING about? I was more befuddled than ever.

I tried to test the waters gingerly so as not to look like a complete idiot, "So, did they say anything about the singing part?"

"Singing?" she wrinkled her brow in confusion, "They didn't say anything about singing. Didn't you read the email?"

Email!? What email?! I am SO out of the loop.

"Um, no. I don't think so," I was beginning to panic now. Maybe I had missed some crucial information about how this audition worked. "What did it say?"

"Strange," she mused, "Everybody gets an email."

Great!!! Now everyone but me would have a foot up because they got this amazing, mysterious, insider email. Hmmmmmm.

I tried to piece together all the bits of information bouncing around my mind. I vaguely remembered the website mentioning something about a tasting contest for a new kind of soft drink. Maybe part of the audition was to try and make a sales jingle for this new product?

No, that didn't make any sense.

When the girl left to go back outside, I began chuckling softly, half in despair and half in amusement. Maybe I had misinterpreted the entire purpose of this event. Maybe this was just some sort of soda tasting convention!

I put on the outfit anyway and sighed, "Well, if this Rich guy needs help passing out fountain drinks, I'll give him a hand."

I just felt foolish for driving all this way for nothing.

As I marched back outside, fitted in my little soda pop ensemble, I decided to be honest with Rich.

"Excuse me," I said, "I am completely willing to help pass out drinks if you need help, but I am just a little bit confused. I thought this was a singing audition."

He didn't say anything for a solid second, studying me closely. "You mean," he paused, "You're not from the modeling agency?"

My eyes widened with understanding.

"No!" I blurted.

Rich immediately burst into a fit of howling laughter. He doubled over, slapping his knees, tears pooling in his eyes. "Come here, everybody!" he cried out, wheezing and struggling to breathe, "Come look at this girl!"

He pointed at me as the other members of the crew began to materialize.

"I told her to put on an outfit, and she did! But she's not from the modeling agency!" Others joined in the laughter, and

I began giggling as well, overwhelmed by the ridiculousness of the situation.

"This is the funniest thing that has ever happened on this show!!" Rich said, wiping away tears, "This is going on the outtakes!"

I wasn't quite sure whether to be flattered, humiliated, or amused. I quickly decided that this was one of the coolest things that had ever happened to me and thanked God for such an awesome morning.

After the laughter died down, I politely declined their offer to join the modeling agency and went to change back into my original outfit. The "real" models had begun to arrive by now, and since I was basically a pro at this point, I instructed them on what they needed to do.

It's kind of neat to be a model instructor if I do say so myself.

I found my mom, and we shared a good chuckle as we sat and waited for the auditions to officially begin. Before long, one of the directors approached us and asked if he could have a seat. At our invitation, he plopped on top of the picnic table beside us. He looked like an oversized little boy sitting there, legs crossed, elbows on his knees.

He introduced himself and expressed his appreciation for my air-headed antics earlier that morning, and we all laughed again.

Then the craziest thing happened—he started talking, like really talking.

He skipped right over ordinary small talk and started pouring out his soul. He began telling us about his fears for his failing marriage, his quest for spiritual truth, intimate details about his background, and his ongoing struggle with depression. Every once in a while, he would stop and shake his head, confessing, "I have no idea why I'm telling you all this!"

It was as if God had cracked open some pent-up dam of emotion hidden within him, and he couldn't help but overflow onto us — a couple of complete strangers.

We did our best to listen as he talked for three straight hours while we waited for my turn to audition. We were able to share the Gospel with him, as well as God's ability to redeem any marriage. He listened with rapt attention as we explained God's life-giving hope and the stability and forgiveness he could find in Christ. Though, to our knowledge, he did not accept Christ right then and there, he seemed to truly appreciate our input. He thanked us over and over again, promising to think about everything we had discussed. When I finally got up for my turn in the audition booth, he pulled out his phone and ordered a James Dobson book my mother had recommended to him.

I walked into my audition feeling as if I had already been awarded the "golden buzzer." Somehow God had used my silly mistake to bring His light, and hopefully healing, to a wounded soul.

Isn't this just like Jesus? He takes over our earthly bloopers, and they end up on Heaven's highlight reel. Our "accidents" become His opportunities. He uses a pair of skinny jeans and a soda pop shirt to mount a rescue operation. I suppose if He can use death to kill death, there's nothing He can't redeem for His glory and our good.

You may be wondering what happened during my actual audition. This type of traveling studio did not host a live judge panel. Instead, there was a small room where you recorded yourself for judges to evaluate later. Heart pounding, I stepped into the tiny cubicle and tapped the screen to begin. A very intimidating recording of the head judge appeared, informing me that I had precisely one minute to impress him. If I was done before the allotted time, I simply had to push the big red button, signaling the end of the recording.

I got this, I breathed. Introduce myself, sing, push the big red button. Easy peasy.

The introduction and singing part actually went pretty well, as far as I could tell. The problem came when I was done a few seconds early and had to push the red button.

I couldn't find it anywhere.

I searched frantically around the room, trying not to look too distraught in front of the camera's ever-watching eye.

Button, button...HOW HARD CAN IT BE TO FIND A GIANT RED BUTTON!?

I ran my hands along the wall, desperate, trying to keep as much eye contact with the camera as possible.

WHERE ARE YOU, BUTTON!?

I don't know how long I looked, but when I finally located the scarlet circle hanging a mere foot from my face, I slammed it hard with my palm. My breath came in shallow gasps as I lingered in the tiny room, stunned and humiliated that I had been outwitted by the easiest part of the entire audition. There was no way a judge would select a candidate who had bumbled around the recording booth, looking completely lost.

I slowly exited the room, shoulders drooping and confirmed my email address with the attendant. Much to my chagrin, they assured me that my file had been uploaded.

They did graciously offer me the chance to submit an additional audition, which I eagerly accepted. This time, however, my voice cracked loudly during the middle of the song.

As I trudged back to tell my mother the grim news, I was flooded with realization. Even though I could not have failed more miserably in my original intentions for the morning, the day as a whole could not have been more of a smashing success!

I set out to make something of myself, but God graciously foiled my plans and used my blunder to make much of Himself.

God is not concerned with how many people know our name. He is concerned with how many people know His name because of us.

In our work and our ministries, we must be careful not to confuse popularity with true prosperity and attention with true achievement. While it is possible to be widely admired and still have a genuine impact, we can never settle for simply having the approval of a large audience.

Our Internet "influencer" driven world makes it easy for me to equate notoriety with accomplishment. Our society literally measures success in "likes."

The highest pinnacle of achievement in our culture is no longer a great scientific discovery or humanitarian effort, but a little blue checkmark beside your name on social media, announcing to the world that you are "liked" enough to matter.

Our children are growing up believing the lie that all they have to do to be successful is to get enough people to "like" them.

We must never confuse a desire to be liked with the desire to make a real difference in the world.

I am reminded of a passage of Scripture where Jesus has reached the height of His earthly fame. He enters Jerusalem to a wild crowd of enthusiastic fans, who basically organize a spontaneous parade to celebrate Him. People are ripping branches off trees to wave at Him, ripping off their coats to lay on the road, so His donkey's hooves don't have to touch the ground. They're so loud the Pharisees are panicking and begging everyone to be quiet.

And what do we find Jesus doing? Is He basking in the

applause, perhaps doing the "elbow, elbow, wrist, wrist," parade wave, blowing kisses to the crowd?

Nope.

He's crying.

"And when He drew near and saw the city, He wept over it." (Luke 19:41)

The Hebrew word used here indicates that He isn't just leaking silent tears. He is weeping loudly.

Why? Because these people who were shouting His praises, who were giving Him what every human craves, were completely missing the point.

These people liked Him a lot, at least for the day.

But they didn't know Him. This group of exuberant admirers thought Christ was some kind of military superstar who had come to organize a rebellion against Rome. They didn't understand that He had come to bring peace to their souls rather than peace to their country.

As He wept, He cried out,

"How I wish today that you of all people would understand the way to peace. But now it is too late, and peace is hidden from your eyes." (Luke 19: 42, NLT)

Christ explains that because they did not recognize Him as God in the flesh, their end would be destruction.

And it broke His heart. It broke God's heart to be "famous" but not really known.

God does not measure success in Instagram likes, Twitter followers, or in reaching celebrity status. God measures success in souls added to His kingdom, not in numbers added to His Facebook group. He doesn't desire distant admirers or members of His fan club.

He didn't buy us with His blood so we could "like" Him. He

died so we could *have* Him.

"Christ suffered for our sins once for all time. He never sinned, but He died for sinners to bring you safely home to God." (1 Peter 3:18, NLT)

So go ahead and dream big dreams—dream of packed-out stadiums and sold-out concert halls.

Dream of them filled with people whose eyes have been opened to the wonders of Christ.

"For am I now seeking the approval of man, or of God? Or am I trying to please man? If I were still trying to please man, I would not be a servant of Christ." (Galatians 1:10)

I may not have become a rock star that day I tried to get famous, but I got to do something better. I got to share Jesus with someone whom God gave His life for.

Even one ransomed soul is worth more than all the likes and retweets in the world.

P.S. When someone tells you the location of a red button, PAY ATTENTION. It could either save your life or rescue you from public humiliation.

2

The Inverted Mohawk

WARNING: The following contains graphic details of what may be the worst hair disaster in recorded human history. It is not for the faint of heart, those who spend their days googling the latest hair trends, or those who flinch at the slightest misplaced bobby pin or fly-away bang.

Actually, I take that back. If you invest *any effort into your hair,* then you absolutely have to read this story.

In fact, if you have ever had *any hair on your head at all,* then you should read this story.

I have ALOT of hair. I stand by a claim I made in college, "My hair could feed five bald men's heads." They printed this quote on the back of the school newspaper. They must have believed me.

Occasionally, I think I should have a separate driver's license or ID card for my hair since it takes up so much time and space.

When my curls implode or snap a hairbrush in half, it's difficult for me to believe that this mop on my head does not have a mind of its own.

Sometimes, having so much hair is fun. "Crazy Hair" day in high school was always the best because I could simply let my hair be itself. Parting crowds and audible gasps would accompany my walks through the halls. Stunned students would comment, "That is NOT your real hair!!" And timidly inquire, "Can I...touch it?"

Other times, having so much hair is not so fun — like when you become an adult and realize it is no longer acceptable to run a brush through it a couple of times and let it bounce around like a tumbleweed on steroids.

As a child, I was completely uninterested in my appearance. I refused to brush my own hair or pick out my own clothes. I could not fathom why anyone would want to waste their time in front of a mirror when a world outside was filled with things like lightning bugs and soccer balls.

All this changed, however, upon entering high school. I became acutely aware of the existence of a stunning creature known as the human male and conscious of a not-so-stunning creature known as the "The Social Ladder."

I was suddenly discontent with my standard tightly-gelled, barely-controlled ponytails. I envied the other girls who chatted easily with boys while flipping their shiny, straight locks over their shoulders. I wanted to experience the foreign phenomenon known as "running one's fingers through one's hair." I had never been able to do this, and it looked like a satisfying experience. Most of all, I wanted to fit in. I wanted to be beautiful.

As a result, I developed an unhealthy obsession with my weight and began spending countless wasted hours in front of the mirror, examining and re-examining my already petite figure. Thoughts that had been previously occupied with discovering ways to stand out became fixated on counting calories and finding ways to look more like everyone else. In summary — I was utterly, completely miserable.

With my sixteenth birthday on the horizon, I suddenly discovered the answer to all of my problems in a miracle procedure which I lovingly called "The Anti-Perm." The beautician would apply the same solution used for a normal perm on my hair. Instead of tightly curling it, however, the beautician would set the solution to wrench the curl out of my hair, leaving me with the shiny, smooth locks of my dreams — or so I hoped.

I remember my anticipation as I entered the salon and pondered the new life now ahead of me. I would be able to woo the finest gentleman with a single swoosh of my newly-freed neck. Heck, with all that extra weight gone from around my head, I might even lose a few pounds. Maybe it would help me run faster!!!

I held stock still as the hairdresser meticulously applied enough tinfoil to my head to enable me to pick up several local radio stations. I was so excited that I tried hard to ignore the horrible smell that began radiating from beneath the foil.

A scent that can best be described as a combination of sulfur and battery acid began wafting from my hair. Initially, it was bearable, but as it grew in intensity, I started to gag. My eyes and my throat burned. Even now, I shudder to think about it. Whatever they had brewing on my head could have been swapped out with tear gas and used in chemical warfare. I thought I might throw up, or pass out, or both.

Sure, perms smelled bad, but were they supposed to smell THIS bad!? I began having serious trouble breathing. In desperation, I called the beautician and asked if this was normal, but she merely shrugged off my question.

How did people STAND this?! Did they ask to be sedated every time they got a perm?

I was on the brink of throwing in the towel and pleading for the awful stuff to be removed when the thought of my long, straight hair stopped me. I was so close to having the hair of my dreams! How could I quit now?!

I gritted my teeth and determined that if other ladies could do this every month, so could I! I squeezed my eyes shut and alternated between holding my breath for long periods of time and taking small gasps of air through my mouth. To distract me from the discomfort, I fantasized about the awed reactions I would most certainly receive from my friends when they saw my new do! Perhaps small, woodland creatures would begin to sing as I walked by, as they did for all the princesses in the movies.

"Count the cost of beauty!" I told myself, "this is going to be worth it!"

Somehow, I made it through the allotted time for the solution to set without fainting. I have never been so happy to have my hair washed in my entire life! I gulped in large, sweet, lungfuls of fresh air and swung my feet impatiently as the beautician poked and prodded my head, preparing me for the final reveal.

Unfortunately, I did not have much time to examine myself in the mirror before I had to rush away to play a soccer game. On the drive to the field, I ran my hands repeatedly through my new lightweight hair. It was indeed a delicious feeling!

I strutted into the locker room filled with the self-confidence that such a marvelous hairstyle deserved and lamented the fact that I would have to pull it back for the game.

I can still replay the events of the next few moments in my mind as if they happened yesterday. (If you grow weak at the knees at the thought of hair disasters, now may be the time to stop reading.) As I leaned over the sink and slowly swept my hair back into its traditional tail, enjoying the extraordinary smoothness under my fingers, I was struck with an unusual sensation.

Near the crown of my head, the hair felt strange. Still soft but somewhat prickly — like freshly cut grass or peach fuzz. It almost like I had a ...buzz cut. The words lingered ominously in my mind as I leaned in closer to the mirror and let my eyes fully absorb the horrible truth.

There, right down the center of my head, starting with where my bangs should have been, was a 2 to 3 inch-wide strip of hair that had been shaved nearly to the scalp. It looked like someone had taken a man's razor and let her rip right down the middle.

Yes sir. I had a mohawk, an INVERTED MOHAWK.

How had this happened!?

I definitely would have noticed if she had taken a razor to my head!!! Wouldn't I!?

Maybe I was just imagining it!

With a trembling voice, I straightened and began walking around the room, inquiring, "Um guys, does it look like I have a buzz cut to you?"

After much inspection and awkward rubbing of my head, my teammates determined that I was indeed the recipient of some strange sort of mutilated buzz cut.

I had never even heard of such a thing occurring!

How does someone go to get their hair straightened and come out with an inverted mohawk!!!?!

It was preposterous! Ridiculous!!

In the midst of that locker-room madness, as I generously offered my teammates the chance to feel my freshly shaven noggin, I realized I had a choice to make — fall into despair or embrace the situation.

I burst out laughing.

I had been trying so hard to achieve a certain standard of beauty that I'd starved and nearly suffocated myself, and this is what I got — the world's first, and hopefully last, inverted mohawk.

I marveled at God's wonderful sense of humor.

He couldn't have me wasting His time on things of no value, so He stepped in and mercifully sabotaged my fruitless pursuit. Though I don't think I completely understood or appreciated what He was trying to teach me at the time, that summer was the last I spent in dangerous obsession over my physical appearance.

Slowly, He began melting away my false preconceptions of beauty and replacing them with His eternal perspective.

Becoming truly beautiful is less about conforming to the cultural archetype of a beautiful woman and more about conforming the whole of our lives into the image of one Man — the God-Man.

It's more about the incarnation of a Divine Personality than about the embodiment of a certain hairstyle, posture, or makeup technique.

If you have ever met a truly beautiful person, you remember. You remember because you walk away from the encounter thinking less about how that person appeared and more about the way Christ made an appearance through that person.

I received one of the highest compliments of my life from a stranger on an airplane. The stranger, named James, had the unfortunate luck of being trapped next to me for several hours on a long flight. James was not a Christian and had never really given much thought to the matter. I sought to change that quickly. He listened intently as I went on for hours about the identity and deity of Christ and how this all-important truth changes everything. During a pause in the conversation, he shocked me with the following admission, "You're beautiful when you talk about Jesus."

My mouth dropped open. "The way your eyes and your whole face lights up, I can really tell how much He means to you." I will never forget the sincerity in his voice and the impact his statement has made on my perception of beauty.

We are the most beautiful when we are the most consumed with Christ.

As Leslie Ludy puts it:

> *When a woman [or a man] finds her satisfaction and joy in Jesus Christ, she reflects His breathtaking valor, glory, beauty, and splendor. Others notice Him shining through her eyes, reflected in her smile and radiating from her*

demeanor — no matter what may happen to her physical body. [1]

Does this mean we should burn our hairbrushes on the altar of self-sacrifice? No.

Trust me. My bedhead would do nothing to advance the Kingdom.

Instead, we need a reversal of priorities.

Before we evaluate our waistlines or our hairlines, we need to evaluate our resemblance to our Redeemer.

Ephesians tells us that growing in Christ looks like taking off an old set of clothes and putting on a new outfit that makes us look like Jesus.

"Put off your old self, which belongs to your former manner of life and is corrupt through deceitful desires, and to be renewed in the spirit of your minds, and to put on the new self, created after the likeness of God in true righteousness and holiness." (Ephesians 4:22-24)

How can we begin to look like someone we don't know? Trying to imitate Christ's style without knowing what He looks like would be like trying to paint a stranger's portrait.

Wanna be beautiful?

Study the Christ, get to know the ins and outs of His extravagantly Divine personality. Learn the ways of His love and ask Him to fill you up to overflowing with His Presence.

Then and only then can we be truly beautiful because we will shine with a Radiance that comes from beyond ourselves.

"So all of us who have had that veil removed can see and reflect the glory of the Lord. And the Lord—who is the Spirit—makes us more and more like him as we are changed into his glorious image."(1 Corinthians 3:18, NLT)

Oh, and just for the record, my mom and I went back to the hair salon to get an explanation for my mysterious mohawk. The staff did not seem at all phased and explained that their customers' hair is frequently burnt off when the chemical solution is too strong or stays on the hair too long.

So that terrible smell I endured? — It was literally my hair being incinerated inside of a make-shift, tinfoil pressure cooker on my head. Burnt hair smell is the worst!!!

They didn't even offer me a refund, and I didn't really care.

I ROCKED that inverted mohawk. Most of the time, I was forced to do some version of the bald man "comb-over" do. Sometimes, just for fun, I would spike it up.

It took until I went off to college for my hair to return to normal length, and by then, I had learned my lesson.

Though I do sincerely hope that you never have to learn the same lesson in this particular fashion.

3

Hot Dog. Train. Midnight.

I'd never ridden on a train before. I didn't even know they still transported people. It turns out they happen to be the cheapest and most efficient means of getting a person across the country to visit a beloved sister.

Plus, it looked like fun.

So a few years ago, I bought myself a ticket and anxiously wheeled my purple suitcase out on the train platform. I couldn't help but imagine that I'd stepped back in time as the shiny locomotive poked out of a distant cavern, rattled over the Potomac, and pulled to a triumphant, squealing stop a few feet away from its handful of passengers.

Feeling quite like the children from *The Chronicles of Narnia*, I clunked up the steps and was immediately impressed by the size and design of the riding car. The seats were twice as large as airplane seats, much more squishy, and put plenty of room between yourself and the next passenger — not that I had much to worry about in that area. Only a small fraction of the seats were taken, and most passengers were surrounded by a wide berth of 10 or so empty chairs.

Normally, this would have disappointed me. I am always up for new people and new adventures; however, I was mostly interested in surviving today.

Throughout my life, I have gone through periods of what I might politely label "mental unrest." A more accurate term would be "mental implosion." I suffer from a strange form of obsessive-compulsive disorder that manifests itself primarily within the hidden recesses of my mind. I don't obsess over color-coding my closet or immaculate floors. I obsess over complex metaphysical nonsense.

In a single afternoon, an untruth or difficult question could burrow its way into my mind and detonate. My sense of soundness and ability to reason is hopelessly fractured. Emotions run haywire, hard lines of truth become blurred. Basic functions like breathing become difficult. Although God graciously delivered me from this particular episode and has been helping me to turn this tendency into something positive, the few weeks surrounding my train ride were some of the roughest of my entire life. I had barely slept in days. My family hoping this trip and the train's newness would help clear my mind and allow me to sleep for at least a few hours.

I had just settled down into my assigned seat and begun pulling out my writing utensils when a man's deep voice boomed down the corridor, reverberating through the entire train. Startled, I peered around the edge of the seat and noted a middle-aged man with stiffly gelled hair making his way down the aisle. He laughed boisterously, made loud jokes, and interacted noisily with nearly every person he passed as if they were old friends and part of some exclusive train club. His voice was notably laced with a thick Russian accent.

Whether it was a divine revelation or a simple deduction of

how things normally roll in my life, I instantly knew that this man was going to be sitting right beside me. Sure enough, he ended his thunderous parade directly in front of me, pointed to the vacant chair to my left, and proudly declared that this was his seat. As I adjusted myself to allow him to slip past, I noted the finger-width, gold chain jingling about his neck (similar to those worn by members of the mafia) and the unmistakable scent of alcohol emanating from his person. I stifled a laugh. I would be getting an adventure after all. God certainly knows how to cheer me up.

I felt a little of my sense of adventure returning to me as the man settled down and began making rather loud small talk. My standard pattern of engagement with seatmates is, to begin with a basic chat about "religion" and then suck them into a discussion about the identity of Christ and, eventually, the Gospel.

Today, however, I was feeling a little hesitant. Was this man even sober? Did he speak English well enough to understand what I was saying? Most importantly — could God even use me right now?

This fragile girl, with the shaken faith and the broken mind.

I whispered a prayer for strength, and without really meaning to, slipped into the general trajectory of my conversations. Before long, we found ourselves in the midst of a full-blown, honest discussion on the Person of Christ. The man described himself as vaguely religious, the sort that believed major religions such as Judaism, Islam, and Christianity were equivalent in nature and ultimately worshiped the same God.

Three hours later, we were still talking.

He asked some very candid, engaging questions and seemed genuinely interested in what I had to say. I learned that he

23

worked for the United States Department of the treasury and was on vacation to visit a friend a Chicago. Though he didn't make any immediate decisions, he at least appeared to put some serious thought into the matter, and I could only pray God had planted some seedling truth also, that he would be able to recall any of the previous night's events the next morning.

The night was black outside our window when the conversation finally died down, and thoughts of sleep began fogging my vision.

I had pulled out a piece of paper and begun writing with hopes that it would knock me out when the man bolted up in his seat and exclaimed with great enthusiasm, "I go get us some munchies!!!"

"Munchies?" I repeated. He grinned at me like he had just offered me Christmas morning and, before I could protest, began squirming his way out of his seat and into the aisle with a promise to return soon.

I buried my face in my hands. What in the world have I gotten myself into?

I checked my phone to find that it was nearly midnight. Did he mean he was going to get us some food? Now!?

I surveyed the otherwise silent cabin to find the lights off, and everyone else sound asleep. He was going to wake up the entire train. I scooted deep in my seat, hoping to melt into the cushions. Within a few minutes, he had returned, grinning wide, arms loaded with greasy food and fountain drinks. He must have gotten the midnight special. More likely, the chef was so happy to see someone at this hour that he had given it all away.

My new friend proudly plopped a giant sausage/hotdog-like thing and a bag of potato chips onto the seat tray before me.

"Oh....thanks," I said, trying my best to look grateful.

I stared at my hotdog, and it stared back at me. Giant, train hotdogs in the middle of the night are not my forte.

I tried not to be ill.

"Eat, eat!" he encouraged, chowing down noisily on his own portion.

I REALLY tried not to be ill.

"Dear God," I prayed, "Please let me be able to take at least one bite."

We had made such progress in our conversation, and he was trying so hard to be generous. I didn't want to offend him by not at least tasting the abominable thing. I closed my eyes and tentatively nibbled at one end of the bun.

"You see Avatar?!?" he suddenly burst between bites of hotdog.

"Um no....," I tried to make sense of his bizarre question, "Do you mean the movie? If so, no, I haven't seen it."

His eyes lit with some apparently wonderful idea, and he began pulling his smartphone from its hiding place.

"You watch Avatar!" his enthusiasm grew as his fingers frantically scrolled through the phone's contents for the film.

"Um, that's ok!" I tried to shrug off his insistent suggestion, "I don't really need to watch it. I'm good, really."

In moments he had the movie playing and was excitedly shoving the phone in my direction.

"Here you watch!" He pressed the warm plastic into my hand.

"Um, that's really ok," I said and tried to shrug it off with a grin, handing the phone back gently.

"You watch!" he pushed it back towards me.

"It's ok, really.."

"You watch Avatar!"

"Nah, I mean...."

25

"You WATCH AVATAR!"

"Ok," I squeaked, quickly accepting the phone and leaning back in my seat, eyes glued to the screen.

Wow, this guy must REALLY like this movie!!!

My decision seemed to content him, and he relaxed to enjoy the rest of his meal while I gave him the occasional encouraging nod.

As I sat there, overwhelmed by the pungent scent of midnight hotdog and relish, trying my best to pay attention to the movie about strange, blue creatures played out on the tiny screen, I realized what a marvelously absurd situation I had found myself in.

I was on a train at midnight, being forced to eat a hotdog and watch Avatar on my seatmate's cellphone.

I decided that this was definitely one of the best moments of my life so far.

I even got out my phone and began discretely texting a few friends for the pure joy of it. "Can't talk now, on train, Russian man, hot dog, Avatar. Will explain later."

It always amazes how God knows exactly what we need when we need it and often brings it to us in the most creative, unconventional packages. I hadn't even been looking for adventure, and He had sent it to sit down in the seat beside me. I couldn't miss it!

Looking back on the experience, I can reflect on God's goodness not only in giving me a good laugh but in teaching me a few life-altering lessons.

First of all, never assume that you are too weak or too broken for God to use you.

If I would have paid a little more attention to the Biblical narrative, I may have noted the innumerable accounts of God using extremely messed up people to do extremely marvelous things.

The Apostle Paul was frustrated by a lingering impediment he simply referred to as his "thorn in the flesh." When he asked God to remove it, God said no, explaining that He meant for Paul's weakness to be a portal for His power.

"My grace is sufficient for you, for My power is made perfect in weakness." (1 Corinthians 12: 9)

Though we should not use this as an excuse for spiritual apathy, we should never assume that we are "too far gone" to be of use to God.

As I began speaking to my new friend about Jesus, I noticed an interesting phenomenon sweeping over me. The truths that had been unraveling themselves in my weather-beaten brain began slowly adhering back themselves back together. What had seemed so muddled in my mind became perfectly clear as it rolled off my tongue and into the light.

As I defended the deity of Christ to this searching man, I found I was also defending Him against the doubts warring within myself. Outside the confines of my internal confusion, I could plainly see that what I was claiming to be true was actually true. Though I wasn't completely through the wilderness yet, the act of verbally expressing unchanging truths about the character of Christ had a profoundly healing effect on my soul.

When you are going through a dark season, and your faith is floundering, do not avoid opportunities for Christian fellowship or to teach the Truth of God's Word. Instead, purposefully seek out these opportunities. Spoken truth is one of the most effective weapons we have for combating the lies and mental fog the enemy often throws our way.

Even if you have to preach to yourself, do not give up the practice of speaking the truth about who Jesus is. The unalterable truth of His Person will be the anchor that holds you through the storm.

Second, never assume that a person will be unreceptive to the Gospel.

We've all done it — passed over the opportunity to share Christ with someone due to some physical attribute or apparent social status. Perhaps they have spiked purple hair—tattoos of deathly objects and unutterable sayings covering every square inch of skin. Enough facial piercings to set off a metal detector. Maybe they just seem disinterested.

When we choose not to share Jesus with someone because of our preconceived notion about their receptiveness, we are grossly misrepresenting Christ and undermining the Gospel.

Jesus is for EVERYONE.

Jesus NEVER allowed a person's social status to stand in the way of sharing His love. This Son of God was the Guy who called vertically challenged tax-collectors down out of trees, broke every "religious" norm to have a chat with the town harlot, and enlisted former prostitutes as front runners in His movement for holiness.

It is not our job to decide who will be receptive to God's message. It is our job to preach the Truth faithfully and without discrimination.

Once, on a plane ride, I had an incredible conversation with an older Hindu man. Though I had initially assumed that he wouldn't want to talk with me, he shocked me with his eagerness to hear about the history of Christianity. As the plane landed, I was struck with the urge to offer him my Bible. I immediately rejected the notion since my Bible at the time was patched together with pink, polka-dotted duct tape and covered in multicolored cards which included multiple pictures of kittens. Surely, I thought, this man would never want this brazen manifestation of girly-ness. However, the urge would not leave me, and I half-asked, half-croaked if he would like to have my Bible.

After some assurance that I was serious, his eyes lit up with excitement, and he eagerly accepted the book. He thanked me repeatedly all the way through baggage claim, and I continued watching him as he walked away, affectionately cradling its brilliant cover like a precious treasure. I was nearly moved to tears by this man's passion for the bright pink, polka-dotted Bible that I nearly hadn't offered him.

Whether or not we are aware of it, we are constantly surrounded by people eager to scoop up and cradle the Gospel. It's not our job to decide who will be receptive to the truth. It's simply our job to share.

I like author Bob Goff's rule for choosing the people with whom we share the Gospel. He wisely says, "Love everybody always."[2]

What greater way can we show love to another human than to die to our fear of rejection, and share the life-transforming message of Christ — even when it's awkward and seems unlikely to bear fruit.

Jesus specializes in the unlikely convert.

I bet no one but Jesus would have taken the chance to recruit a tax collector.

I bet no one but Jesus would have taken the chance to recruit a bunch of uneducated fishermen.

I bet no one but Jesus would have taken the chance to recruit a man whose life purpose was to hunt down and kill Christians.

I'd say that turned pretty ok.

Who can you take a chance on today?

As for my Russian friend and me, I managed to sleep a little on the train that night.

We reached my destination before my new companion had awoken. So, I scribbled a note on a small scrap of paper, daring him to investigate Christ further. I tucked it carefully into the back of his seat pocket next to the infamous smartphone.

Whether or not he woke up with any memory of the previous day and our conversation,...I will never know.

But I do know that I took the chance.

Thank You Jesus for taking a chance on me.

4

I Lost My Monks

Did you know airplanes have batteries?
And if these batteries die, mechanics have to fly in giant-sized jumper cables to restart them?

I did not.

When an official announced that our flight would be delayed due to a dead airplane battery, I was half-horrified and half-intrigued. I imagined little repairmen crawling over the plane lugging cables as big as fire hoses, kind of like Oompa Loompas.

No one else seemed quite as enthused.

This announcement was met with the typical, nonsensical outrage that accompanies flight delays. I feel like the anger experienced in airports should have its own special classification. We call anger experienced in cars "road rage." Why can't we call the indignation of a delayed air traveler "airport animosity" or "flight fury?"

Anyway, while my fellow passengers moaned loudly and filed grumpily into line, I grew secretly excited. This would allow me to chat with lots of new and interesting people.

I closed my eyes and said a silent prayer that God would allow me to share Him with someone. Maybe I could even have lunch with a delayed passenger.

The instant I opened my eyes, I felt a light tap on my shoulder. I turned to find a kind-looking woman smiling at me. She had deep brown eyes and was wearing the traditional Hindu bindi. "Would you like to have lunch with me after we get through the line?" she asked sweetly.

My heart pounded furiously as I grinned and answered without hesitation, "Yes! Yes, I would!"

We shared a lovely chat over tacos, musing extensively about life and Christ. As we boarded our finally-fixed plane, she asked me to keep in touch and continue to pray for her.

I settled down in my seat, marveling over God's amazing ability to put people together. I was actually disappointed to find that the seat beside me had remained empty, even after everyone had boarded.

My loneliness was a cure when a bumbling commotion at the front of the plane caught my attention. A curly-headed preteen girl noisily clunked into view, lugging a large, black instrument case. She seemed completely oblivious to the stares of the entire plane as she awkwardly clunked along under the guidance of her assigned stewardess. I grinned broadly, thrilled to find she would be my new seatmate.

"Aubrey" was 12-years-old, without the slightest hint of shyness, and on her way to music camp for the summer. She immediately began chattering loudly away about all the adventures she had already encountered this morning on her journey through the airport. "I got a video of an old man eating a BANANA!!!"

"Whhhhhattt?" I tried to act impressed.

"I call it, 'Old Man Eating Banana.' Do you want to see it!? It's

SO funny!"

She pulled out her tablet and began watching a 10-second video of an elderly gentleman consuming a banana while waiting for his flight. For some reason, she found this absolutely hysterical and watched

It on repeat in both fast and slow motion. Each showing was followed by the question, "Did you SEE that?"

I didn't think it was funny at all but found her enthusiasm for the clip highly amusing. I am also pretty certain the entire plane could hear our every word and wonder what was so hysterical about this fellow and his banana.

"Did you SEE how he chews it!?" She practically shouted.

"Yeah, so funny," I whispered, attempting to calm her down.

"Oh, MAN, this is great!" She wiped tears of laughter from her eyes.

"Yeah," I patted her shoulder, wondering how I could change the subject before this poor man faced any further public humiliation.

Without warning, Aubrey gasped and whirled to face me with wide eyes, "Did you see the monks?"

"I did," I whispered back, "They're actually on this plane."

"What!?" she yelped, leaping to her feet, "Where?!"

"No, no, no," I hissed, urging her to return to her seat. My cheeks burned with embarrassment.

I used some highlighters to draw her a cartoon of a banana wearing sunglasses to entertain and distract her.

It was a *very* interesting flight.

It became even more interesting when the speaker system crackled with a new announcement — a storm had temporarily shut down the Atlanta airport. Rather than land, we circled our destination in the air for an additional two hours. This triggered another round of "flight fury" as everyone realized they would miss their already-rescheduled flights.

At least I had an entertaining seatmate. Aubrey and I developed quite the friendship as we repeatedly looped through the thunderclouds. Though I was relieved when we were finally able to land, I was reluctant to say goodbye to my new friend. She must have liked me, too, since she later listed me as a job reference on a resume. A few years later, I was contacted by a company inquiring if I thought she would be a good employee. I mean, who wouldn't want to hire someone who could entertain herself for hours with a video of a man eating a banana? She'd never complain about being assigned to a monotonous task. We're talking instant, "employee of the month," material here.

As we trundled down the ramp and into the terminal, I made sure Aubrey was safely passed off to her assigned guide before pausing to stare in shock and horror at the bedlam surrounding me.

Have you ever been in a crowded building when someone pulled the fire alarm? Or been in a high school hallway after the final bell rings? Or been caught in the middle of a stampede of angry water buffalo?

It was kind of like that. Since all flights had been grounded for hours, the terminal was basically a zoo of caged passengers foaming at the mouth from flight fury. If they didn't start opening the runways soon, people would grow fangs and start eating each other.

I studied my useless boarding pass. I had missed my connecting flight by hours. What was meant to be a quick morning trip had turned into an all-day saga. The coworker who was supposed to meet me in Chattanooga must have been so confused. Somehow, through the madness, I discovered that the help desk was located at gate B18.

I braced myself and plunged into the torrent of tourists barreling through the center aisle of the terminal.

It was sort of like white water rafting through people. I had only gone a short way when I felt a firm tug on my sleeve. I whirled around and found myself nose to nose with one of the Buddhist monks from my flight.

He had a panicked expression and held out his wrinkled boarding pass for me to see. Someone had written "B22" in bold sharpie and circled it for him. He must have recognized me from our flight and reached out to me for help amidst the chaos.

"B22!! B22!!" He shouted, tapping his ticket passionately with each distinctly pronounced syllable. As I studied the boarding pass further, I noticed he had also missed his connecting flight. He would need to come to B18 with me.

"B22! B22!!!" He continued to yell frantically.

"No, no, no," I tried to console him gently, "B18, WE need to go to B18."

He studied me for a second, then looked back down at his ticket and continued his pointing and shouting routine, "B22!! B22!!"

"No, no," I tried again, "B18."

"B22!! B22!"

I decided to try a different tactic.

"Don't worry!" I leaned in close, speaking loudly so he could hear me over the chaos, "I will help you!!!"

His shoulders wilted in relief under the orange robes. "Oh, tank ooo, tank ooo," he breathed.

He then took me completely off guard when he threw one of his arms around my neck and leaned into me, resting his head on my shoulder. He was a small man, no taller than me, and we

35

started wading through the chaos in this position.

I barely knew this little man, ye the had his arm wrapped around me, and clung to me like a lifeline. He, nearly naked, lugging his little white sack containing all of his belongings, me with my wheeley purple suitcase. We made quite the pair, my monk and I. At that moment, I was supremely grateful that God had made me only 5 feet tall.

We had gone a little ways when I realized there had originally been two monks. "Where's your friend?" I tried to ask.

I could tell by his confused expressions that he didn't understand my question. I whipped my head around but couldn't catch any glimpse of brilliant orange amongst the throngs of people. All I could do was hope he found his way to the help desk.

"West woo! West woo!!" my monk friend suddenly began shouting and nearly jumping up and down with enthusiasm, "West woo! West woo!"

"West woo?!" What is he talking about? Realization dawned on me as he began frantically pointing at a set of doors down the hall. He didn't say a word before leaving my side and bolting for the doors.

The restrooms!!!

I followed, and before he rushed inside, he dropped his white sack at my feet with the unspoken understanding that I would watch over it for him.

So there I stood outside the men's restroom at the Atlanta airport, awkwardly waiting for my monk, watching over his small satchel. I tried to smile and look natural as the hordes of people thronged past.

Suddenly the other monk emerged from the crowd and came immediately to my side. He must have been trying to follow us. This man was much younger and spoke much better English.

I was able to gather that they were headed for some sort of religious convention.

I greatly enjoyed the joyful reunion of the two friends as my original monk emerged from the men's room. Together, we trundled in our strangle little caravan towards B18.

As we took our place at the rear of the endless line, my throat began to burn. I had just gotten over a cold, and though I didn't want to abandon my new friends, I knew that I wouldn't be able to make it through the line before needing a drink. There was a Long John's Silvers a few gates away, and I decided to make a quick pit stop.

I turned towards the two men and commanded, "You stay right here. I'll be right back." The older man blinked at me in confusion. "You stay here!" I said a little louder while pointing to the ground, "Right here!"

"Right here! Right here!" he repeated, gesturing towards the floor as I had done. Satisfied, I smiled and bolted for Long John's. After snatching up a quick soft drink, I turned and wheeled as quickly as I could back towards the helpline.

When I reached B18, I halted abruptly, horrified. Though the line hadn't progressed much since I left, there was no sign of my friends. I spun around, searching desperately, but could find no sign of brilliant orange robes in any direction. My chest clenched in fear. Had they thought I ditched them and then rushed off to find gate B22? Were they wandering around lost, worse off than when I found them?

I began to wheel down the line, inquiring noisily of everyone I passed, "Have you seen my monks!?"

No one seemed to have noticed the presence or sudden absence of the two men. I groaned, frustrated.

Aggravated and angry with myself for having left the line, I marched quickly to B22, hopeful I would find them there.

The gate buzzed with eager passengers but no monks.

The song title, "I Left My Heart In San Francisco," came to mind, replaced with the words, "I Lost My Monks At Gate B22."

The Atlanta airport terminal is massive. I had almost no chance of relocating them in the post-storm pandemonium.

Defeated, I turned and wheeled solemnly back to the helpline, praying that my friends had found someone else t to help them. The line moved faster than I anticipated, and I was soon holding a brand new boarding pass. An elderly Canadian woman in line behind me was told she would have to spend the night in the airport, so I let her borrow my cellphone to call a relative. I have no idea what she was saying since she spoke in French, but it made me feel a little better about losing my monks.

I kept waiting for them to show back up with their little satchels and their friendly smiles, but they never appeared. By the time I landed in Tennessee, it was late at night, and though I was bursting to tell my coworker all about the day's adventures, I was still concerned about the fate of my new friends.

Sometimes I still wonder about my monks. I worry they're still out there, wandering in circles around the Atlanta airport terminal, holding up their tickets and shouting, "B22," to anyone who will listen.

Of all the craziness that surrounded my trip to Chattanooga, the memory I reflect on the most often is the moment when the monk wrapped his arm around my shoulder.

It was a gesture of such innocence, such trust. Something best friends would do. This man had known me for approximately twenty seconds, yet he possessed no fear that I would reject his embrace.

Wouldn't it be great if we all approached God like that monk approached me? I had done absolutely nothing to prove myself trustworthy, yet he threw himself at me with abandon.

God has done absolutely everything to prove that He wants to draw near to us, yet we so often cower away from His outstretched arms.

We hide in the corner, trembling, "You don't want to touch me! You don't know how dirty I am."

In his book, "Gentle and Lowly," Dane Ortland explains:

> *We naturally think of Jesus touching us the way a little boy reaches out to touch a slug for the first time— face screwed up, cautiously extending an arm, giving a yelp of disgust upon contact, and instantly withdrawing.*[3]

This false image of a cringing Christ could not stand at greater odds with the Savior we see striding along the shores of Galilee.

Ortland goes on to say, "The cumulative testimony of the four Gospels is that when Jesus Christ sees the fallenness of the world all about Him, His deepest impulse, His most natural instinct, is to move towards that sin and suffering, not away from it."[4]

My pastor recently delivered a sermon that helped me see where I had doubted Christ's sincere affection and desire to be with me. Pastor Jim explained how we often view our Father God like an angry sports coach — impossible to please, constantly benching us at the slightest mistake or fumble.

We should instead believe our Father when He assures us that He loves us like a parent who cherishes a beloved child, like a groom who gushes over his bride on their wedding day.

"We don't have to perform for a God who already adores

us as His adopted children. I am not saying we turn apathetic and lazy, but I am saying we get to stop trying to impress God. God wants to be with us. And that reality produces anything but apathy."[5]

When we are in Christ, we never have to cower in the corner. Even when we have messed up again, find ourselves trapped in the vicious cycle of addiction, feel our affections being dragged away from the truth, we can "come boldly to the throne of our gracious God. There we will receive his mercy, and we will find grace to help us when we need it most." (Hebrews 4:16, NLT)

When we are in Christ, we should "Expect love, love, and more love." (Jeremiah 31:3, MSG)

Like my monk friend, I don't want to be hesitant or embarrassed to throw my arms around Him in my times of deepest need and confusion.

Sometimes in this life, we get lost. Christ knew this would happen. It's why He calls us sheep. Getting lost is just what sheep do. It's also why He describes Himself as the Good Shepherd who promises to leave a whole flock of sheep behind to find even one little, lost lamb.

Don't be ashamed to be the lamb. If you find yourself lost and confused, just hold up your boarding pass and start shouting. Christ will come for you.

And when He comes, don't be afraid to lean into Him. He's the Only One who can lead you home.

...And He will be much, *much* better at guiding you than I was at guiding my monks. He won't leave you to get fast food or anything.

Also, if anyone has seen my monks or has any idea what

happened to them, I would greatly appreciate it if you could let me know. Every time I pass through an airport terminal, I stop in front of Gate B22 and hold a brief moment of silence for them. Maybe you could do the same and ask God to send some lost people your way.

5

The Day I Hugged Jesus

I met Jesus in Florida.

He was using a microphone and sporting a pair of shiny, silver shoes.

Before you go crying heretic on me, allow me to explain.

A few years ago, I hit upon a dry spell in my Christian walk, more of a desert, actually.

I felt distant in my love relationship with Christ, disappointed by my continued state of singleness, and disillusioned by my inability to accomplish anything that I felt was significant.

When I saw that I had a day of free time scheduled for a business trip to Florida, I knew exactly what I would do with it.

A local Floridian theme park held a daily passion play, featuring a live reenactment of Christ's death and resurrection.

This may have been more than a little crazy, but I decided I was going to take myself straight to the source, to the only one who could fix my dehydrated soul. I was going to meet "Jesus," or at least the actor who played him at the park.

Yes, I realized that this actor, whoever he may be, was not some sort of deity and not the real Jesus.

Yes, I realized that the presence of the Holy Spirit, alive and active in my soul, was more real, more intimate, than any physical interaction with another human being.

Maybe I was wrong, but this fragile human being who navigated this fallen world with her eyes and with her ears really just wanted to experience Jesus with her eyes and with her ears, even if just for a moment.

I was desperate, and I knew God never turns down a request for more of Himself. So fueled by this slightly insane hope, I hopped into my beat-up rental car, plugged the address into my GPS, and began my journey towards the heart of the city.

My plan went something like this —

1) Get into the park.

2) Find out where "Jesus" is.

3) Go there.

That was pretty much it.

I prayed fervently during the entire drive, explaining to God that I knew this fake Jesus wouldn't be real, but that maybe, just this once, He could use this fake Jesus to show me how much the real Jesus still loved me.

I am not recommending that others participate in such a crazy pursuit, and I knew that Christ's love for me would remain the same despite the results of my grand experiment. I couldn't shake the desperate hope I felt rising within me that something incredible was about to happen.

Tears were slipping down my cheeks before I ever even entered the gates. Despite the park attendant's doubts concerning my sanity, I was granted a ticket. I immediately began pushing my way through the thousands of visitors to the site of the passion play. It was such a hot day that the park had rigged the stands with a sprinkler system to spritz the audience periodically. So I sat —steaming, wet, and breathless, waiting to see "Jesus."

Though the performance was very well done, and I was moved, I wasn't granted the opportunity to connect with "Jesus." The cast disappeared immediately after the show, and I tried not to be deeply disappointed. I waited until everyone else had left to make my exit and stood wondering what to do now that my "plan" had fallen through.

That's when I heard the singing.

The music was being piped through a loudspeaker system, and I began wandering to find the source of the sound. I had my answer in moments as I stumbled into a replica of Solomon's temple courts.

And there was Jesus.

He was singing while walking back and forth in front of the temple steps, occasionally venturing into the crowd for a more personal touch.

I had a brief, internal argument about where to sit before sliding onto a sunlit bench. As crazy as this may sound, I didn't want "Jesus" to notice me because I made a scene or picked a spot on the front row. I wanted him to notice me because God sent him to me.

My feet bounced up and down nervously, tears streaming down my cheeks. I decided it would be best to close my eyes. I also decided that I had probably lost my mind.

A sudden warmth settled on my shoulder.

I froze. My eyes snapped open.

"Jesus" had walked over and put his hand on me.

I was so stunned I didn't know how to react, my head still hung towards the ground. He lingered for the briefest second and had begun to step away when I dared to raise my head and look him in the eye.

"Jesus" stopped, stopped moving, stopped singing, and just stared.

He looked at me, REALLY looked at me, and seemed genuinely moved.

"Do you know that He weeps when you weep?" He asked, voice thick with emotion.

I tried to smile and nod, but you probably couldn't tell since my face was swollen to roughly the size of a watermelon from all of the crying.

I was breathless, completely wrecked. It was wonderful.

"Jesus" retreated to the front and continued with his routine, but it wasn't long before he paused from his normally scheduled programming. He closed the distance between us in a few strides and slid onto the bench in front of me to face me. "This is not God's plan B for your life. This is His plan A," he said confidently before reaching to grab my hand and give it a gentle squeeze.

I almost melted. He stood and began addressing the crowd before beckoning me to stand. I sprang to my feet without hesitation.

Then "Jesus" pulled me close and put his arm around my shoulder. I don't think he anticipated the intensity of the bear hug I threw his way. I wrapped my arms around him and squeezed him tight, resting my head on his chest like a little kid.

Remember this, I thought, breathing in every tiny detail.

"This is how near I am to you always. I hold you just like this, all the time." His voice boomed over the crowd.

45

I didn't want to let go.

The best part was when he finally released me, I could tell he didn't want to let go either.

I wish I had words to describe the wonder of that encounter adequately, but I have found that words fall short.

God had answered my desperate and somewhat foolish prayer more extravagantly than I ever could have imagined.

He didn't have to do that. My Father has already shown me more love than I could ever fathom by sending His real Son in real flesh and blood.

But He did it anyway because my God is just THAT good.

I ended up staying at the park until it closed, and you wouldn't believe who was walking out at the same time I did. Me and "Jesus" talked for such a long time they had to get security to re-open the gate to let me out.

Am I fanatical enough to believe that this paid actor, dressed up in what may or may not be historically accurate wardrobe, was actually Jesus Himself?

No way.

Do I think that Jesus Himself used this man to reveal a piece of His heart? Did He want me to know that He hadn't forgotten about me, that He still loved me, and that He still had an amazing plan for my life?

Absolutely.

Do I think it's a coincidence that out of the thousands of people in the park that day, He chose me to pull up to the stage, to speak with face-to-face, and to comfort in such a personal way?

Not a chance.

Do I think that Jesus loves me any more than He loves those other thousands of people whom He didn't call out personally?

Nope! In fact, I believe this experience proves the opposite.

Jesus doesn't love me or want me, one iota more than He wants any of His children.

I think He shared this experience with me so that I could share it with you. So I could share Him with you. I don't have a beard, or a robe, or cool sandals. but I do have a keyboard and wi-fi connection, and I know this —

Even when you don't see it, and you don't feel it, and your soul feels as dry as a desert...

Jesus weeps when you weep. FOR REAL.

He has a plan for you, and He hasn't given up on you. FOR REAL

Jesus is as close as a bear hug and a whisper in your ear.

FOR REAL, AND ALWAYS.

You don't have to get in a car and drive to Florida to meet Jesus. You can meet Him right where you bend your heart and open your mind in prayer.

RIGHT, WHERE YOU ARE IS WHERE HE IS.

You are not an inconvenience to Him. He doesn't mind keeping the "park open late" for you.

He's just been waiting for the day when you'll stay so long inside the gates of prayer. He'll have to have security come and unlock them to let you out.

I am no farther away from Him at this very moment than I was all those years ago, wrapped up in an actor's embrace.

The Bible assumes as a self-evident fact that men can know God with at least the same degree of immediacy as they know any other person or thing that comes within the field of their experience. The same terms used to express the knowledge of God are used to express the knowledge

47

of physical things. 'Oh, taste and see that the Lord is good.' 'All thy garments smell of myrrh, and aloes, and cassia, out of the ivory palaces.' 'My sheep hear my voice.' 'Blessed are the pure in heart, for they shall see God.'... What can all this mean except that we have in our hearts organs by means of which we can know God as certainly as we know material things through our familiar five senses? [6]

Today, I am not headed towards a first century-themed park to find "Jesus," but I am still offering up a desperate prayer, "Father, open the eyes of my heart that I might see you and know you, right here and right now."

If you're feeling far apart from Jesus, if you're wondering whether or not He still cares, do what I do — reach out your arms and squeeze. You can maybe even whisper, "I know You're there."

6

The Great Mortarboard Malfunction

I t was finally here.

Four years of study-packed days, nearly sleepless nights, and being pushed to the brink of my intellectual, physical, and emotional limits (pretty sure I have stretch marks on my brain) had all added up to this moment—my college graduation.

As I stood tall and proud on the side of the stage, anxiously awaiting my name to be called, one prominent thought rolled through my mind, "Please don't trip."

My alma mater is a very prestigious academic institution that takes events such as graduation very seriously. All the senior's movements had been carefully calculated and diligently rehearsed. There would be no cowbells, obnoxious whistles, or attention-seeking stunts pulled by over-enthused graduates. Oh no, this ceremony would be characterized by an attitude of thoughtful reflection and a quiet solemnity brought on by the newfound weight of our post-collegiate futures. A distinguished American war hero, a man for whom I hold deep respect, was slated to deliver our commencement address.

Before that morning, my life had been consumed with keeping

my mind in order, carefully organizing my thoughts on a page or in a presentation. Today, all I had to do was keep control of my feet as I walked across the stage, proving to all the world that I was now a full-fledged adult, ready to enter the workforce.

It couldn't be too hard, right?

I was all too painfully aware of my specific propensity for tripping, also for spilling hot drinks and running into inanimate objects. Once when giving a campus tour to some prospective students and their parents, trying to convince them to attend our school because of the quality of its education and graduates, I had walked face-first into a giant pillar. In the days leading up to graduation, I had half-jokingly mentioned to several friends that I would most likely fall while receiving my diploma. We enjoyed a good chuckle over this imagined scenario. However, inside I understood that this was a genuine concern.

In high school, I had played Wendy in our drama department's production of Peter Pan. It was opening night, and we had made it to the final scene — what was meant to be the emotional reunion of the Darling children with their parents.

The mood was set. The lights were dimmed. I attempted to climb gracefully through a fake window and into my on-stage "bedroom" and instead managed to get my nightgown snagged on the window frame. While the actor playing John worked desperately to unhook my dress, I tried to act natural, as if standing there unable to move was a part of the program.

After a few moments of awkward struggling, I assumed I had been released and took a bold step forward.

I was wrong.

WHAM!! The nightgown jerked me back like a small dog in a leash, and I smacked hard onto the stage, flat on my face.

Though I recovered quite quickly, rolling onto my side and

cupping my chin in my hands with a cheesy grin, my stunt had completely ruined the emotion of the moment.

Now, years later, as I stood seconds away from my moment of collegiate glory, I reminded myself to concentrate on my footing. At the sound of my name, I ascended to the stage with small, delicate steps. As it turns out, I should have been less worried about my feet and more concerned about my head.

All went smoothly as I managed to make it halfway across the stage without falling on my face. I felt fairly confident when a board member with whom I am personal friends stepped forward to wrap me in a bear hug.

It was a great hug, so great that the intensity of the hug combined with the voluminous nature of my hair sent my hat flying across the stage. The crowd erupted into laughter as I stumbled backward to collect it and hastily smash it back onto my head.

How embarrassing! I thought perhaps my moment of indignity was over until I noticed the painfully pale expression on the Provost's face. He was grimacing and pointing with urgency back towards the stage entrance. My tassel had somehow detached from my hat and now lay like some sort of hideous, golden squid near the stage entrance. Before I could move, the college President swished forward under the bulk of his colorful regalia and kindly grabbed it for me.

The crowd lapsed into hysterics as we tried to maintain an air of composure while he handed me my diploma.

I didn't even bother to reattach the tassel as I began what I hoped would be a redemptive, graceful exit. When the college Chancellor stepped forward to hug me, the unthinkable happened—my hat flew off AGAIN!!!

The laughter reached a fever pitch as the Chancellor held

up a hand and graciously offered, "Allow me!" I decided to embrace the madness fully and stepped forward to the front of the stage with the attempted poise of pageant queen awaiting to be crowned. When he carefully placed it on my head, I threw both my arms into the air in a gesture of victory. The crowd went wild!! You would have thought I had just been awarded an Olympic Gold medal.

As I attempted to exit the stage for the third time, I was greeted by our prestigious commencement speaker. He was laughing SO hard that TEARS were literally streaming down his face. At this point, I had abandoned all attempts at poise. I had never met this man before, but I was in a hugging mood, so I thrust out my arm for an embrace.

"Oh no, you're not!" he breathed between guffaws, lifting a hand to stop himself from being the third person to de-crown me.

And you know what...I hugged him anyway.

And THAT, ladies and gentleman, is how I made an American military legend cry. I should probably put this accomplishment on all my future resumes...without mentioning they were tears of laughter.

I could also mention that out of all the graduates, they chose my picture to post as the commencement advertisement on the school website. I won't mention the picture was of the gloriously absurd moment in which I was "crowned" with my mortarboard.

The school photographer later presented me with a cd of pictures documenting the entire incident. He had hand-drawn a picture of my hat and lovingly labeled it "The Great Mortarboard Malfunction."

Before I made my failed attempt to receive my diploma with some amount of respectability, I had been pretty proud of myself.

Graduating from college, especially Patrick Henry College, is not an easy thing to do. Perhaps somewhere in my klutz of a brain, I had begun giving myself too much credit for my triumphant navigation through the world of academia.

There's nothing wrong with feeling good about your accomplishments. The problem arises when we begin to believe that we are the source of our own success.

There is a wonderful book called " A Turtle On A Fence Post,"[7] where the author discusses his rise through the heights of success. In describing this book, author Joseph Stowell says, "If a turtle is on a fence post, you can rest assured that someone put him there. It took a power beyond his own to place him on that lofty perch."[8]

Isn't this a perfect description of all of our lives? We're all just tiny little turtles, under the care of a Great Big God who has picked us up and carefully positioned us in places of honor we don't deserve. Stowell explains:

> *If you and I are ever going to experience Jesus in the way we long to experience Him, we need to learn how to get beyond ourselves and our achievements to get all the way to Him...When we are blessed, we need to master the response that takes that spark of joy we feel about ourselves and lets it explode into the joy of celebrating His preeminent provision and grace in our lives.*[9]

Micah 6:8 instructs us, "Don't take yourself too seriously—take God seriously." (Micah 6:8 MSG) God has downloaded each of us with a powerful and wonderful set of gifts and abilities.

Something to be excited about! However, we will only reach our maximum potential when we fixate on the magnificence of God rather than the extent of our own giftedness.

There is such freedom in learning to take God seriously instead of ourselves.

When we take ourselves too seriously, we are constantly obsessed with our image and our accomplishments. We will be trapped in a comparison game with the world that, in the end, is fruitless.

Jenny Allen says in "Nothing To Prove" that while we are wasting our time trying to prove ourselves to God and outperform other people.

> *All the while Jesus is saying, I want to free you from your striving, free you from your doubt, free you from your pride that cares more about achieving something than you receiving something. I am enough. So you don't have to be.* [10]

When we learn to take God seriously, we are finally freed to wholeheartedly enjoy the One who will never let us down.

My final piece of advice is to ALWAYS wear bobby pins when graduating. ALWAYS. You can thank me later ;)

7

God's GPS

B ack in ancient times, before Siri could talk, people used something called a "GPS" to get around. You would mount the little mini-computer onto your windshield and manually type in your destination. To update its database to include the latest roads, you actually had to use this thing called a wire and plug it into a physical computer. I know, it sounds crazy!

The result was a lot of wrong turns and outdated information. I am saying all this because it makes me feel better about making such a horrible mistake.

I would love to say that the blame for the whole situation lies entirely with faulty technology, but really, I should have known better.

At least the first part of the mishap wasn't my fault. Who knew that my faithful old GPS would direct me to a Jewish temple instead of the pizza place I had punched in?

Now, the second part in which I failed to realize that I had reached a place of worship instead of a pizzeria and began walking around inside asking where I could order my food...

that was probably my fault.

The third part in which I finally wised up to the situation, yet became incredibly fascinated with the building and decided to explore it instead of leave..that was definitely my fault. (The kind secretary who found me wandering about the halls and gave me directions to a real restaurant was a lifesaver. She also looked at me like I was an alien.)

For the fourth part, where I decided that I had not yet creeped out quite enough people and that I should stay and watch a bit of the child's program that was happening that evening...the blame also lies entirely in my court. Who knew that a junior, dramatic production of the book of Esther could have such an emotional effect on a person? If I had known that I would suddenly be overcome with compassion for an entire room of people who had no idea who Jesus was, burst into tears, and run out the back door (nearly bulldozing my new secretary friend), perhaps I wouldn't have stayed.

Then again, knowing what I do know about God's gracious method of placing purposeful detours in our lives, perhaps I would have hung out a little longer and sobbed my way through the Second Act.

Looking back, I could brush off the incident as a laughable yet simple mistake, a mere distraction that kept me from getting my pizza on time. Or, I could see it as a God-ordained opportunity to learn something I couldn't have otherwise.

In our attempts to follow God's will, we are often too quickly frustrated when we find ourselves in situations that don't seem relevant to His larger calling on our lives.

God, I know You want me to be a doctor, so why do I have to take this year off grad school to work so that I can pay for next year's tuition? Why aren't You providing for me?

God, I know You want me to be a wife and mother, so why am I graduating from college as a single woman with no romantic prospects? Did I mishear You?

God, I know You put this dream in my heart to work in foreign missions, so why am I stuck working retail in Wisconsin? What is the point of this in-between time?

In these moments of confusion and distrust (which I experience often), we need to consider the possibility that we have been asking the wrong questions.

God's priority is never so much about what we are "doing," as is it about who we are "becoming."

We get so hung up on charting our life progress regarding society's benchmarks like education, career, and recognition that we miss God's grading system entirely.

God's tape measure is not wrapped around the size of our achievements. Instead, His ruler is curled around the shape of our spirit and the growth of our likeness into the Image of His Son.

He didn't send Jesus to make climbing the corporate ladder a more expedited process. He sent Jesus to draw us into the life-giving process of growing oneness with Himself.

When I worked as an admissions counselor, I often had long conversations with distraught high school seniors who desperately wanted to follow God's will for their lives but weren't sure what that looked like. They were frozen with indecision about schools and majors, afraid that one wrong choice would forever dislodge them from God's will.

The words of comfort God gave me to share with these applicants remain relevant for both students and "grown-ups" in all walks of life.

"God is not so much concerned with what you are going to

'do' when you grow up, whether you become a doctor or a lawyer or a teacher, as He is concerned with who you are going to 'be' when you grow up.

Will you be a man or woman of character? Will you be a man or woman after His own heart? When we focus our efforts on our intimate connection with Christ and becoming more like Him, all those other details about schools and majors and careers will simply fall into place. It may take time, but we can trust that He will work everything out for His glory and our good. God is never late, but He is never early."

For those of you feeling stuck or sidelined and wondering how in the world you ended up at a "temple" instead of a "pizza place," remember this–

More than God wants you to be a college graduate; He wants you to be a student of His heart.

More than God wants you to have a successful career; He wants you to have a vibrant, thriving relationship with Him.

More than God wants you to look accomplished; He wants you to look like Jesus.

This perspective shift on God's priorities completely changes our view on life's little detours. Instead of meaningless rerouting times, you can remember that your situation has been crafted specifically to make you more like Jesus. Without each new experience, even the ones you feel are extraneous, you might miss a crucial aspect of intimacy with Him.

The one goal in life which we cannot afford to miss is intimacy with Christ.

Where is your life headed? Now you have an answer. Jesus is your horizon. And because He deigns to make us one with Himself, this horizon is not only beautiful but also accessible. Jesus already went the distance, and now He takes hold of you to bring you there.[11]

The timing of the "temple" incident couldn't have been more perfect. During that season of my life, I felt completely side-tracked from what I felt were God-given goals. I was confused about where He was taking me. It appeared we were headed in the opposite direction of my preprogrammed plan for success. In my personal Bible studies, I was repeatedly drawn to Solomon's construction of the Temple and God's promise that He would help Solomon complete his dream if he would simply stay "strong and courageous" and continue to "do the work" no matter what happened. (1 Chronicles 27:20) Engraved in giant letters into the temple's foyer I "accidentally" visited was a verse about Solomon completing his temple. It was as if God was whispering in not-so-subtle terms, "Nothing about your situation is a mistake. Even this GPS malfunction was preprogrammed to let you know that I am still guiding your every step. Just take courage and remain faithful to My call, and I promise I will complete the dream I planted in you."

In Christy Nockels' book, "The Life You Long For,"[12] she encourages believers to seek *intimacy* with Christ above *achieving* for Christ. Nockels is a world-famous worship leader and songwriter. She was living the life of her dreams yet still found herself grappling with feelings of discontent. The wisdom of Psalm 37 rescued her from her own obsession with success, "Delight yourself in the Lord, and He will give the desires of your heart. Commit everything you do to the LORD. Trust Him, and He will help you. He will make your innocence radiate like the dawn, and the justice of your cause will shine like the noonday sun." (Psalm 37:4-5)

Christy realized she had been chasing her "cause" — her callings and dreams — above chasing Christ Himself. When she began to reorient her life around delighting in Christ and His love for her, she was finally able to find rest in releasing her dreams into His all-knowing hands. She reflected, "The One who placed all these gifts and talents and dreams in us — wouldn't He be the best promoter of our cause that ever existed?" [13]

If you find yourself frustrated with life's latest detour, ask yourself, "Have I put chasing my calling above chasing Christ?" This doesn't mean life won't hurt or that all seasons will be easy, but it does mean we can find rest in the One who wrote our stories before we were born.

As Nockels says, "The most beautiful part of trusting in God as your provider and your promoter is that, not only do you walk into dreams that He's already prepared in advance for you, but you also begin to experience a satisfaction in His love that none of your previous wants and desires and dreams could ever come close to fulfilling." [14]

So slow down, friend. Breathe. Stay strong and courageous! Resist the urge to throw your spiritual GPS out the window and follow your own impulses. Just because you haven't arrived at your intended goal yet, doesn't mean you aren't on the right track.

Jesus is right here. You aren't missing a thing.

8

My Not So Cinderella Story

L et me start by clarifying that no one saw anything.

This information will greatly decrease the scandalous rating of the following story. If you are reading this anecdote and happened to be present at this unfortunate event and DID see something, please do not tell me. I would like to go on with my life under the illusion that I have retained at least some shred of my dignity.

If Cinderella were to be re-written based on my personal experience, the royal ball would have ended on an unexpected twist. The damsel in distress would not have lost her shoe. She would have lost her dress, or at least the back part of it.

NOTE: Please read the following in your best Shakespearean accent until you can no longer contain your laughter. It will make for a much more enjoyable experience.

I never felt more like a princess than the night of the Christmas Ball during my sophomore year of college. The event coordinators had rented out a gorgeous dance hall complete with sparkling chandeliers, moonlit verandas, and a live string ensemble to provide us with the perfect "royal" atmosphere. My dress even LOOKED like the Cinderella dress from the cartoon movie!

It was light blue, long, and be-studded with the perfect accent of pearls. Surely no hot-blooded gentleman would be able to resist asking me to dance.

As we entered the hall, I remember being overwhelmed by its general "fairy-tale-like" feel. Indeed, the night began to progress much as I had imagined. A few male friends asked me to dance, and I willingly obliged, tangoing and twirling incessantly about the floor like a graceful swan.

A princess must always twirl. I think that is an official rule written down somewhere.

Wildly romantic thoughts swayed through my mind with the music. Perhaps my prince was watching me now, hopelessly entranced by my swanlike-ness. Overcome with passion, he would ask me to dance, and we would be engaged by the stroke of midnight.

When a particularly good friend of mine asked me to dance, my romantic fantasies were in full swing, imagining that my would-be prince was watching from somewhere.

I remember clearly that the dance was a tango, and I had to concentrate on executing each step with precision.

Slow, slow, quick, quick, slide.

Oh dearest prince, does thou noticeth me?

Slow, slow, quick, quick, slide.

Won't thou come and rescue me?

Slow, slow, quick, quick, slide.

Sweepeth me off of mine feet?

Slow, slow, quick, quick...

RIPPPPP!!!!

The noise was startlingly loud.

I immediately recognized it as the sound of tearing fabric and chuckled inwardly.

Some poor soul's dress had just ripped.

That poor girl.

My legs felt freer than ever, moving uninhibited by the confines of my gown.

Wait a minute...

Suddenly, I felt a rush of air tickling me in areas that moments before had been shrouded by the safety of blue silk. Areas that should NOT have been exposed to open air. I froze.

The poor soul was ME. The unthinkable had just happened. My dress had just ripped straight up the back while I was standing in the middle of a crowded dance floor.

Mortified, I held perfectly still, unsure of the extent of the damage and unwillingly to cause further exposure. One of my hands was still raised in a half-turn position, sort of like I was doing the robot. I stared speechless at my friend, eyes wide as saucers.

He stared back, brow raised in confusion and concern. Thankfully, he was facing me from the front and was oblivious to my perilous situation. Everyone around us had continued to dance as if nothing had happened.

This was a good sign. I half-whispered, half-hissed, afraid to attract attention to the spectacle of my accidental exposure, "My dress ...just...ripped." He paled, "What should I do?"

Still frozen in my robot-like state, I hissed, "Give...me...your jacket!" He quickly and silently removed his suit coat, and I threw it over my shoulders. Thankfully, he was tall enough that the jacket covered any unsuitable areas. I made an awkward turn towards the lady's room and began what could accurately be described as the shuffle of a wounded penguin. As I waddled my way through the crowded dance floor, I prayed desperately that no one had noticed anything regretful.

The cardinal rule concerning women and restrooms apparently applies everywhere, even fancy balls. Within minutes, nearly the entire female population of the ballroom had joined me in the bathroom, ooohing and aaahing over the impressive damage done to my once-beautiful gown.

How had I done it? How was this sort of thing even possible outside of the movies? I could only shrug.

My klutziness was simply that spectacular.

In a single, misplaced step, I had crushed my romantic hopes and lived out one of every woman's worst nightmares. There would be no fairy-tale ending tonight, only cowering in a bathroom and wishing that I could puddle into the floor and die. My fairy godmother would be ashamed.

As I later mused on the situation, I would conclude that the real root of my problem was nestled much deeper than my remarkable clumsiness. I am so thankful for a Father God who knows exactly how to make me laugh and is good enough to reach down and get my attention when intervention is needed.

You see, the part of the story that I didn't tell you is even more shameful than a ripped dress. At this point in my life, I lived exclusively within the confines of my college's vibrant Christian community.

It was truly wonderful. We had daily chapel services filled with solid Biblical teaching and sincere worship. In and out of class, I was immersed in rich theological discussions and was constantly challenged with new and exciting ideas.

I felt like a little sponge, eagerly soaking up all of the goodness. Somewhere along the line, however, a subtle shift began to occur in my attitude. It happened slowly, like a gradually tightening corset. My hubris-laced dress had squeezed the air from my lungs before I even realized I was suffocating.

Instead of responding humbly to the wealth of knowledge being thrown my way, I skipped the whole "storing things up in my heart" bit and let my new expertise go straight to my head.

I began to take pride in my new status as a theologian, feeling as if I belonged to some sort of elite "holier than thou" club. Some part of me believed that I must have earned my admission into this upper echelon of Christianity. I became so concerned with climbing the ladder of social status that I forgot to draw near to God.

Pride is like poison. It crept like quiet acid through my system, corroding everything.

Even in my quest to locate my "prince," I was hoping to find someone who could better my ranking within my Christian circle.

How utterly upside down.

The whole point of marriage is to serve as a living Gospel drama.

There's this thing about the Gospel. At its core, center stage is a cross.

It's not pretty. It's crude, and rough, and blood-stained and stands for what I truly deserve.

Those nails were my fault, hammered through by my own two hands.

The ugliness of my sin somehow reached back through the centuries and pinned Him there.

But it was His love that kept Him hanging there.

The essence of the Gospel is understanding how much we NEED Jesus.

If we ever begin to believe that we need God less than we did at the moment of our salvation, we have begun going backward.

As pastor and author Judah Smith says, Jesus "lumps all of humanity into two groups: people who think they are righteous and people who know they are sinners."[15]

The people who are closest to God's heart are the ones who most clearly recognize that they are unworthy of being there. They are the ones who openly and consistently acknowledge that Christ's righteousness alone has allowed them to draw near.

"The bedrock in Jesus Christ's kingdom is not sincerity, not deciding for Christ, not a determination to serve Him, but a complete and entire recognition that we cannot begin to do it. Then, says Jesus, 'Blessed are you.'" [16]

In my arrogance, I had become like the wayward Jerusalem described in Ezekiel 16.

I had forgotten that He had rescued me from certain death.

Forgotten that God had spoken, "Live!" into my bloody, broken mess of a soul and carried me home. (Ezekiel 16:6)

Forgotten that He exchanged my dirt for HIS perfection and my shame for HIS splendor.

Forgotten that He had clothed me in Himself, that when people looked at me, they saw the handiwork of the Creator, not the created.

I had begun to "trust in my own beauty" and play the spiritual harlot, wooing thirsty souls away from the cross and towards myself. (Ezekiel 16:15)

The lesson of the dress is loud and clear. When we try to clothe ourselves in our own self-righteousness and flaunt it around like a pretty gown, sooner or later — it is going to rip.

We will stand exposed (in my case literally) for who we are — ordinary people in need of an extraordinary Savior.

In retrospect, I'm kind of glad my dress ripped in half. Though I will say, I hope it was a once-in-a-lifetime experience.

Luckily, the gals in the bathroom were able to scrape together about 30 safety pins and several pieces of fabric tape. The makeshift fix enabled me to waddle to a chair in the ballroom and watch the rest of the festivities from a distance.

It was totally worth it.

I kept that dress in my closet until I got married. The jagged, safety-pin-laced scar served as a constant reminder of that not-so-magical night and the enduring faithfulness of God.

"Nevertheless I will remember My covenant with you in the days of your youth, and I will establish an everlasting covenant with you...then you shall know that I am the LORD." (Ezekiel 16:60, 62b)

9

The Snake-A-Nator

A few years ago, on an otherwise mild May evening, my father made the fateful decision to go to bed early. He cracked the window open an inch before crawling under the covers, hoping to draw in the sweet, spring breeze.

Shortly after falling into a fitful sleep, he heard a noise and shifted in bed. His right arm swept across his chest, and much to his surprise, he felt something heavy fly off of him and onto the floor.

The mysterious object landed with a startlingly loud THUD!

He shot up to investigate and stared part horrified, part fascinated, at the invader sprawled out like a slick, rubbery rope on the carpet.

This can't be real, he thought. My wife is playing some sort of trick on me.

As he continued to stare, however, he realized the 4-foot long black snake flicking its nasty, little, forked tongue back up at him *was very real.*

On instinct, he crawled quickly off the end of the bed and shut the bedroom door to prevent it from escaping.

Meanwhile, my mother, who had been snuggled up on the couch reading a book, heard the commotion and came to investigate.

"Tim!?" she cried from the bottom of the stairs, "Is everything ok?"

"Yeah, yeah, it will be," he swallowed, not wanting to sound too alarmed. "...Just don't come upstairs!" he added as calmly as he could muster.

"What's going on!?!?" My mother grew more insistent.

What do I do? What do I do? My father, generally a very brave and manly person, stood paralyzed by the door. He was afraid to take his eyes off the vile varmint for even a moment, fearful it would disappear into a dark corner.

What kind of snake crawls up on a person's chest while they're sleeping?! He thought.

He quickly surveyed the room, scoping out his options for retaliation. His choices were admittedly limited and included several pairs of high heels and a fluffy bathrobe collection.

"We have a snake situation," he announced reluctantly.

My mother — possibly the kindest, most graceful woman in the world — replied in a manner fitting to the situation, "A SNAKE SITUATION!?"

"Don't worry!" my father cried reassuringly. Sweet relief washed over him as the unwelcome creature began winding its way up the bedside table and back outside through the cracked window. "It's leaving!"

"LEAVING!? What do you mean it's leaving!?" my mother shouted in a panic, "Kill it, so it doesn't come back!!!"

"Kill it!?" he quickly scanned the room again for a weapon — any sort of weapon — that could end the unwelcome beast's life. "How am I supposed to kill it!? With a shoe!?"

By this time, my sister had become aware of the epic battle taking place upstairs and decided to join in the shouting.

"You're the man of the house!" she cried, "Kill it!"

Inspired by their cheers, my dad rushed forward in a daring act of brilliance and manly heroism. He crossed the room in two great strides, grabbed the window frame, and brought it down with a triumphant THWACK on the beast's back.

I think there should be some sort of ninja move named after this valiant effort. Perhaps the "snake-otine" or the "exterminator."

The thrill of using the window as a weapon was short-lived as the snake began to thrash around violently, whipping the curtains and letting off a horrendous stench. My father gagged, cringing at the sensation of being bullwhipped by a snake tail. He managed to press down tightly on the frame until he was certain the villain could not escape.

To seal the deal, he grabbed a shovel and ventured out onto the roof. If the neighbors noticed their pastor crawling out onto his roof in his nightclothes and work boots, they never said anything.

Dad said the snake put up a snapping, hissing fight to its very headless and very smelly end.

The stench was so bad my parents had to sleep in a different room that night, but in the end, my father had had won a great victory, and a story for the ages had been born.

After relaying this bizarre encounter to friends and family, my parents discovered that it was not uncommon for snakes to seek sources of warmth at night, even when that source is human. This unlucky beast had simply chosen the wrong man to make his personal heating pad.

The following weekend was Mother's Day, and as a part of her gift, my dad bought my mom an extendable shovel and labeled it in bright red lettering, "Snake a-nator, Extends 2 Feet to Get the Really Big Ones."

As I contemplate this simultaneously horrifying and incredibly entertaining saga in my family's history, I can't help but notice the remarkable parallels between the snake's passage into my parent's room and sin's entrance into our lives.

That's just what sin does to us, isn't it? It creeps up on us when we're least expecting it. We get comfortable in our sanctification, let down our guard for just a moment, and it comes creeping in through the smallest crack, the littlest seam in our defenses. Before we know it, we're cozying up with a terrible habit or thought pattern, wondering how such a monstrous creature has worked its way into the sanctuary of our soul.

We have multiple options for responding to this unnerving situation:

A) We can give in to fear and personal weakness and simply allow the snake to take up residence in our inner lives.

B) We can stand and stare paralyzed, praying that if we simply stare at it long enough, it will go away or disappear.

C) We can KILL IT. Through Christ's victory on the cross, we have been given "everything we need for a godly life." (2 Peter 1:3, NLT) It might take a bit of Scripture searching and some serious crying out to God, but we can rest assured that "The Lord knows how to rescue the godly from temptation." (2 Peter 2:9 NASB 1977)

This snake story reminds me of a startlingly similar situation

71

involving my younger brother. Apparently, in my family, the mark of reaching true manhood is the ability to kill small household pests.

I was driving home from college with my mother when my cellphone rang. The voice on the other end was heavy, panicked. I barely had time to say hello.

"PUT MOM ON THE PHONE!" my teenage brother boomed through the earpiece.

I quickly obeyed and handed the phone over to the driver's seat.

My mom's eyes widened, "Well, kill it!" she boomed back, "BE A MAN!"

Before I continue with this story, you need to understand something fundamental about my brother, Jordan, who was 16 at the time. The term "athletic" is an understatement. Actually, the terms "uber self-confident, super-studly, over-achieving jock" are an understatement. We're talking man-child who can squat twice his body weight, lead his team to four state-cup soccer championships, and kick a 60-yard field goal. There has to be something pretty major to get him riled up.

I only caught bits and pieces of their phone conversation in real-time but was later able to piece together both of their accounts.

"But mom," my brother shouted, "I've never seen a spider like this before! It has yellow stripes, and it's as big as a BASEBALL!! It's so big it not only has legs, it has FEET!"

"It has....feet!?"

"YES, IT HAS FEET!"?

"Just kill it!! Get a shoe and smoosh it!"

"No way am I gonna get close enough to do that!!"

"Just be a man!!"

"....BASEBALL, mom! Big as a BASEBALL!"

My mom gave a long sigh, "Where is it?"

"In the bathtub."

"Well, go into the kitchen, get some of that yellow cleaner from underneath the sink and spray it. It'll make it easier to kill."

"I CAN'T DO THAT!"

"Why?"

"What if it leaves while I'm gone!???!!!"

"Well, hurry!"

Silence. More silence

"What are you doing, Jordan?"

Silence.

"I'm... watching....it."

Silence.

"Kill it, Jordan."

Silence.

"How long till you get home, mom?"

"45 minutes."

"I think I can watch it till you get back."

"Kill it, and I'll get you whatever you want from Burger King."

The sound of rummaging, bottles clanking. "NO YELLOW, MOM! There's NO YELLOW!!"

Desperate rummaging.

Desperate clanking.

"Jordan, just grab something! Anything!"

Very, very desperate rummaging and clanking. "I CAN'T FIND IT!!!!"

The pound of sprinting feet hitting the floor.

Heavy breathing, "It's still there."

"Kill it, Jordan."

"I'm gonna prove it to you. I'm gonna take a picture of it with my phone and send it to Brooke!"

"Then will you kill it?!"

He hangs up the phone. 30 seconds pass. The phone rings again.

"Did you send the picture to Brooke?"

"No....I couldn't get close enough to get a good shot."

"So....does that mean you didn't kill it?"

"Taco Bell. I want Taco Bell."

Sighhhhh.

"It's so big it will SQUISH EVERYWHERE!"

"If you kill it. I will clean it up."

Jordan speaking in his most professional voice, "Ok, Mr. Spider, I am going to give you 'Spider options.' Option A-I smother you to smithereens. Option B-You commit suicide right now. Option C-You disappear and never come back...I'm going to give you fifteen seconds to commit suicide."

Fifteen seconds pass.

"Ok, just kidding, fifteen minutes!"

I put out my hand and demand the phone.

"Hey buddy, you can DO THIS!"

"Brooke...it's as big as a BASEBALL!"

"I believe you. You can DO IT!"

"I'm standing here....looking at it right now...and it's as BIG AS A BASEBALL!"

"Jordan....kill the spider."

There was a dramatic pause, followed by an intense rustling and a WHACK!

"NOOOOOOOO!!"

"I MISSED IT!"

Disbelief. Shock. Terror.

My turn to scream.

"OH NOOOO! Well, get it! Keep going! Don't stop!"

A thudding and cracking and booming.

"Jordan!?... Jordan!?.... What's HAPPENING?!"

BOOM.RUSTLE.BOOM.

A shout of joy, "AHAHAHAHAAHAHAHAHAH! Got YA! He tried to get away, but I caught him on the fly!"

Whooping. Hollering. Screaming.

"Take THAT, son!"

Silence.

Then Jordan said something I won't forget for a long time.

"Wow," he was softer, more contemplative. "It doesn't seem that big now...."

Mom and I shared quite a good chuckle over the absurd situation on the way home. As the miles flew by, it suddenly dawned on me that Jordan's escapade wasn't so abnormal. It's actually very similar to the internal war we wage every day against our flesh.

I am constantly attacked by an army of my own personal "spiders." I'm not talking the hairy, 8-legged, web-spinning kind—I'm talking about something much worse—"pet" sins. We've all got them, trouble areas or nasty habits that seem to creep and crowd the edges of our lives despite our best efforts to exterminate them. For me, maybe it's incessant worry or "performing" my walk with Christ for other's approval. For some reason, I get the idea that since these vices are my "natural" weaknesses, God will understand and allow me to continue my merry way in these destructive habits.

ThankYou Lord for loving me more than I could love myself.

Like Max Lucado says, "God loves us just the way we are. But He refuses to leave us that way. He wants to make us just like

Jesus." [17]

Due to His great love, our Father can only allow us to go on hoarding these repulsive creatures for so long. Sooner or later, these pests will emerge from their "holes" and invade our comfort zones.

One day we'll wake up to discover an occasional indulgence has become an addiction, a vice has become a lifestyle. There will be a snake curled up on our comforter or a spider the size of a BASEBALL in our BATHTUB. Bigger and blacker than we ever thought possible. The infestation dirties even the " cleanest" areas of our lives. We have to choose— stay soiled or face our worst nightmare—death to self.

My knee-jerk reaction is typically something like Jordan's frantic phone call. I look to someone stronger and call on my Heavenly Father, "AHHHHHHHHHHHHHHHHHHHHHH!!!! Help me!! That "pet sin" just turned into a monster!! It's disgusting and big, and it's ruining everything! I can't hide it anymore! What do I do!!!????"

Even though I technically ask, "What do I do?" Deep down, I am really hoping He says, "Don't worry. I'll come and squish it for you."

Instead, He often surprises me with the response, "Put it to death! Act like My child, and kill it! Be an overcomer!"

It's not that Our Father doesn't possess the power to squash sin. He already squashed sin once and for all on the cross. God doesn't actually *need* us. He has just *chosen* to release His power in this world through the voluntary love and cooperation of His people.

Our part in sanctification is not to produce Christ in ourselves but to take up the power His cross endowed and exterminate our earthly selves. In Colossians, we are commanded to, "Put to

76

death, therefore what is earthly in you!" (Colossians 3:5)

No one put Jesus on the cross. He *chose* to be there. "No one takes my life away from me. I give it up of my own free will.." (John 10:18)

In the same way, God is not going to force you onto your cross. Only *we* have the power to choose to die to our flesh.

Just like my mom couldn't reach through the phone and squash the spider for Jordan, our Heavenly Father says, "This death to self thing, it's not something I can do for you. I won't leave you. I'm not going to hang up the phone. But our communication is going to be a little strained until you act with the overcoming power my blood offers."

There are various reactions to this command. One of my favorites is to "pull a Jordan" and stare, paralyzed at the beast hoping that it will go away on its own. "You know, " I rationalize, "I'm just gonna keep an eye on it, and maybe it'll disappear. I can handle this." The obvious problem is that my life will be lived standing still instead of flooding the world with the Light of Christ.

Another one of my favorites is to say, "Ok...I'll do it. But maybe a little at a time." Instead of outright slugging the thing with a boot, I'll get out the bug spray. This approach to sin is also a mistake. A squirming spider is still as bad as a fully alive one. Our fellowship with Christ remains strained in each situation.

The only correct response is, "Yes, Father. In Your strength, I'm gonna step forward and SMUSH this thing!" He shouldn't even have to offer us any incentives. There is no greater reward than unbroken fellowship with Himself.

The next time you find yourself in a staredown with some unexpected, hideous sin, choose courage. Act like the man or woman of God's that you are, gather up your guts, and CHARGE.

Slam down your "window" and hang on tight, even if the enemy puts up a fight and lets off a terrible stink. Then grab your shovel, and END THAT SNAKE.

It is both your destiny and birthright in Christ, to "crush" the head of the enemy. Jesus has already smashed the head of ALL your spiders and all your snakes on the cross. As AW Tozer says, "You have been forgiven, so act like it!"[18]

Jesus is the Only "Snake-A-Nator" we will ever need.

By the time my mother and I got home, the "monster" spider had already shriveled up to the size of a peanut. Its once intimidating legs hung limp and bent. It looked more like a hairy raisin than a fierce predator. I think I actually laughed at loud. I then smiled contemplatively and thought, "Wow, that's how small my sin is ALL the time..."

"And you, who were dead in your trespasses and the uncircumcision of your flesh, God made alive together with him, having forgiven us all our trespasses, by canceling the record of debt that stood against us with its legal demands. This he set aside, nailing it to the cross. He disarmed the rulers and authorities and put them to open shame, by triumphing over them in him." (Colossians 2:13-15)

10

The Rubber Band Miracle

Americans go crazy over the silliest things.

When I was in college, it was all the rage to wear neon-colored rubber band bracelets. When worn around your wrist, these beauties looked like ordinary stretchy bracelets. When removed and thrown onto a flat surface, the bands constricted into distinctive shapes: cats, flowers, dinosaurs, etc.

Children would start conversations by stripping their arms and throwing down their bracelets. Everyone would huddle together, and ooh and ahh while the hidden objects magically appeared. People would trade for their favorites and scour stores for the newest and rarest designs. It was sort of like collecting baseball cards...but in jewelry form.

I knew these bracelets were all the rage, but I was unaware of their supernatural potential until I purchased a package of "Gospel Bands" at a Christian conference out West. The colorful set included shapes like a cross and an empty tomb and was designed to provide a fun and easy way to share the Gospel.

I was soon to head back home and hoped they might instigate

some good "plane" conversation on the return trip. Since obviously, all mature adults wear rubber band bracelets and compare them with their seatmates on cross-country flights. Please tell me you did this too!

The night before my return trip, I carefully laid out each piece on my cheesy hotel bedspread and prayed specifically for the people who would sit by me on the plane the next day.

Sure enough, the following afternoon, we had barely poked our head through the clouds when the young man sitting to my left asked to see what sort of bracelets I was wearing. I was all too happy to oblige and enthusiastically laid out my practiced presentation. Unfortunately, he seemed about as interested in our conversation as I am in repeating 8th-grade algebra.

Discouraged, I settled back in my seat and contemplated whether or not to plug in and watch the movie playing across tiny screens throughout the cabin. The passenger seated to my right, a man in his early forties, had shown no interest in seeing my bracelets, and I was beginning to think the whole thing had been a bad idea.

I had plugged and unplugged my headphones several times when the man reached over and introduced himself. He informed me that I reminded him of his teenage daughter, "Kylie." Kylie was passionate about sharing Christ and very active in her church. Apparently, this man we'll call "Joe" was a Christian and had noticed my little presentation after all.

Though his eyes were alight with pride as he shared about his daughter, his countenance was laced with an underlying sadness. I could sense the weight of a hidden burden tugging at his soul.

I discovered the source of this heaviness as he began to talk about his wife, "Patti." Over the past few months, the normally bright and vibrant woman had succumbed to the ravages of an undiagnosed illness.

What started as a twitch in her feet quickly escalated into an inability to walk or consistently control any part of her body. She became confused and often displayed erratic behavior. Most recently, she had begun losing her ability to speak.

Tears filled his eyes as he described his daily struggle to care for her and the frustration of visiting 17 different neurological specialists, none of whom had any answer for her sudden demise.

I felt sick to my stomach as I imagined the horror of watching a loved one fade away in my arms with no antidote and no answers to offer her.

With no help from the doctors, prayers that seemed to bounce off the ceiling, and friends who had reached their limit in assisting with the ever-growing task of caring for his wife, Joe had begun to feel increasingly and utterly alone.

He seemed, in a word, empty.

As I sat wishing desperately for a way to help him, he announced that the purpose of his trip was a training course that would be held in Shepherdstown, WV.

I did a double-take. "Did you say, Shepherdstown, West Virginia!?"

Amazingly, my tiny hometown was very close to Shepherdstown. The odds of a man from Houston catching a flight to visit this hidden city, hours away from the closest airport, were probably somewhere close to one in a million.

As he recounted stories from his line of work involving harrowing escapes from forest fires and dangerous encounters with wild hogs, I anxiously wondered what God meant to do with this strange connection. Surely, this couldn't be a coincidence. Our conversation continued all the way through baggage claim. After saying a reluctant goodbye, I climbed into my mother's car and immediately told her everything about my new friend.

Her eyes instantly lit up with recognition. "I know exactly where he's going!" She explained that the National Training Center for the US Wildlife Service was located in Shepherdstown. Even better, she knew the man who used to run the center. In her ferocious determination to share Christ's love, my mother resolved that we were going to find Joe, and we were going to have him over for dinner.

A little while later, her eyes widened further. My mother was also friends with the wife of the man who used to run the center, and she was no ordinary woman. Plagued by recurrent and serious illness throughout her adult life, my mom's friend had developed a sort of ministry giving medical advice and referring people to top physicians in the appropriate field. Throughout her health struggles, she had developed a network of connections with some of the nation's top specialists.

A final game plan materialized.

A) Have Steve over for dinner.

B) Get his wife referred to a specialist who could crack the code of this mysterious illness.

As soon as we got home, my mom began making phone calls. Before long, an all-points bulletin was released at the training center for a "Joe from Houston" to call my cell phone. The owner's wife informed us that she was personal friends with one of the nation's most prominent neurologists, as well as his secretary, and would gladly help him get his wife an appointment.

A few hours later, my mother and I were again piled into the car, following our GPS up a windy road to pick up our somewhat amazed dinner guest. Joe seemed more than thrilled to accept our unusual taxi service and trundle off to a near stranger's house.

That evening as we huddled around our family's table, partaking of my mom's sweet tea, and my brother's ridiculous jokes, it seemed as if some of the life was re-infused into Steve's weather-worn soul. He smiled. He laughed. He gratefully accepted the new doctor's information, and maybe for a couple of hours, was able to forget the dark cloud that had been choking out his world for the past few months.

As we waved goodbye for the final time, there were fresh tears in Joe's eyes. This time, however, they were tears of joy and not of sorrow.

As my mother wisely reflected later that evening, "I think he just needed to be reminded that there was still good in the world."

The world itself is not always good, but the God who holds the world in His hands never runs out of goodness, even in our darkest hours.

I think God placed Joe in the seat beside me so I could let him know that his God was still real, that God's love for him was still alive, and that no matter how alone he felt, Joe had not been forgotten.

As Christians, we are often too hesitant to share God's love because we fear rejection or that our means of showing love will be too small.

My encounter with Joe helped me to understand that no attempt to share God's love is a waste.

What if that kid hadn't brought Jesus his lunch because he thought it would be too small? 5,000 people would have gone hungry.

What if Jesus hadn't stopped to talk to that one woman at the well? I mean, her problems were huge, right? What could one conversation do to help a serial sinner like that?

What if I had decided that my bracelet idea was just too silly?

It is impossible to fail when we take even the smallest step to share Christ's love. The only way to fail in showing God's love is never to give it a try.

Unfortunately, I never found out if Joe was able to get Patti in to see the neurologist or if things got any better. We had our third-grade Bible school class send them a huge box of "Get Well" cards but never heard anything in reply.

Even though I have been tempted to feel like our investment in Joe was a failure, I know that Joe saw Jesus while sitting at our dinner table that night.

That's always a win.

11

I Would Kiss You But I Don't Know How

There are many kinds of kisses in this world. This is the story of my first one. It was fairly awkward, unexpected, and exceptionally beautiful.

It was hot in that 7-Eleven parking lot. The mid-August sun beat down on my light blue Buick while I waited for him to finish filling up my tank. I pretended not to stare as he leaned confidently against the car in his fitted white t-shirt, thumbs hooked nonchalantly in the pockets of his worn jeans.

Oh dear goodness, he was very cute indeed.

I had only met the man a few hours ago and was feeling things that I had never felt before. I caught my breath as he slid back into the driver's seat and shut the door.

His hands found the steering wheel, but he made no move to turn the key.

He didn't say anything.

He just looked at me.

Well, not just at me, exactly. He was looking at my lips. AT MY LIPS!!

My mind raced, cheeks flushed, pulse quickened. Is this what someone does when they want to kiss someone!? I don't know! How does one know if one is about to get kissed!?!?

FLASHBACK TWO YEARS

I was laid out on my couch after knee surgery, quite out of my mind on pain medication, and quite starved for male companionship. My sister seized the opportunity and hinted not so subtly, "Hey, there's this cool dude named Kyle who I met on that mission trip this summer. You should ask to be his friend." *Very sneaky.*

I looked at his profile picture, loudly declared, "Oh, he's CUTE!" (I don't remember this, my sister had to tell me later), and pushed the friend request button.

Approximately 2 seconds later, my in-box chimed with a message, "I have a bad memory...Have we met?"

Thus began a decade-long conversation, as I have just now opened my Facebook app and see that I have an unopened message from him.

We talked for two hours that today and for the following two years after that.

He was attending college in Arkansas for early childhood education while I was on the cusp of finishing up a journalism degree in Northern Virginia.

I was wrestling with my post-graduation future and the certainty that God had called me to work for His Kingdom, but the uncertainty of what that looked like.

Kyle was wrestling with a call to ministry but felt inadequate and unqualified for the job.

We talked on and off in a platonic friendship, encouraging one another to follow Jesus and giving general life advice.

He dated other girls, other guys were interested in me, but eventually, our conversations escalated to almost constant chatter. My growing emotional attachment led me to the unpleasant realization that we couldn't go on like this forever.

It wasn't healthy for my closest friend and confidant to be a man on the other side of the country who I would, for all practical purposes, never be able to meet.

My ever-wise mother encouraged me to make a gutsy move that nearly ripped my heart out. I told Kyle that he either needed to find a way to come and meet me in person, or we needed to stop talking.

The following two weeks were horrible. I never thought I would see or hear from him again.

Then one afternoon, as I was by myself in my office, spinning circles in my desk chair, I thought I caught a glimpse of my mother's car pulling up to the front of the building.

I stopped spinning. My dizzied gaze honed in a tall, lean figure in a Razorback cap and work boots that were deposited by the entrance.

He rolled back his broad, muscled shoulders and took a deep breath before beginning the long ascent up the front steps.

My heart stopped.

This was him.

This was Kyle.

I panicked, pruning my hair and checking my outfit. For the first and only time during my employment in that office, I was all by myself manning the phones while the rest of the staff was out to lunch.

Unfortunately, I was in the back cubicle and unable to leave my desk for fear the phone would ring. How was he going to find me?! In my blind panic, I had a stupidly wonderful idea. I started singing.

Here's the crazy thing. During his all-night drive, he had rewritten the lyrics to a popular love song to match our story, and *he* had started singing on his way into the office.

When I heard his voice and saw his smiling face peeking around the corner, I forgot all about the phones and sprinted to embrace him. To this day, no other hug has even come close to topping that one.

My incredibly generous boss was kind enough to allow me to have the rest of the day off, and we nervously piled into my car for the journey home.

I had no idea where to take him or what to do, so as the consummate pastor's daughter, I decided it would be a good idea to take him on a tour of my church. That seemed to go well, and an hour later, we found ourselves in that fateful 7-Eleven parking lot surrounded by the oh-so-romantic scents of gasoline and baking asphalt.

NOW BACK TO THE GOOD PART

The hot car got about ten degrees hotter. He kept staring at my lips, and I kept staring back at him in half awe and half horror.

WHAT WAS I SUPPOSED TO DO!?

If he was going to kiss me, wouldn't he like purse his lips or something? Make some sort of kissing noise?!

2 Seconds stretched into 5.

I can't kiss him! I just met him! What if I'm wrong and he

doesn't want to kiss me, and we just bump noses or something horrible!?

5 seconds stretched into 10.

Am I supposed to purse MY lips!? Do I like wink or something!?

10 seconds turned into a moment of decisiveness.

I swallowed and said with a quavering voice and all the twitterpated courage within me, "I would kiss you right now, but I don't know how."

Immediately he let out a breath of intense relief and nearly shouted, "It's not that hard!"

He dropped his hand from the steering wheel, cupped my cheek in his palm, and pulled my face to his for a brief second before sensing my intense nervousness. "Don't worry," he smiled," There's really no way you can mess it up."

There's also really no need to narrate the rest.

It must not have been that terrible since he decided to marry me a little less than a year later, on only the 10th occasion we met in person.

I have learned a lot about kisses and a lot about love since then.

There are many kinds of kisses in this world...

Love is first kisses in 7-Eleven parking lots.

Love is invisible, I miss you, kisses blown over a thousand miles.

Love is shouting, "Yes, I will!" kisses while he grins up at you from bended knee.

Love is wild joy kisses on an altar with a brand new ring and a brand new name.

Love is first kisses in the dark.

Love is kissing him right in the middle of Walmart just because you can.

Love is bent over kisses in hospital beds after three days of labor and a brand new little person breathing into your chest.

Love is, "Have a great day," kisses with morning breath and crazy, curly bed head.

Love is welcome home kisses, when because of the baby, you still have morning breath and crazy, curly bed head.

Love is kisses of sweet relief because the baby's FINALLY asleep.

Love is salty, teared kisses when you think your heart might break.

Love is laughing kisses when you think your heart might pop.

Love is quiet kisses after prayer.

Love is jumping up and down kisses when Heaven answers.

Love is wishing you could kiss him just this instant when you see him doing something so brave and looking just like Jesus.

Love is kissing him anyway when his dirty laundry covers your clean floors, and he doesn't like what you made for dinner.

Love is kisses of encouragement.

Kisses to be strong.

Kisses when he looks so darn cute and doesn't even realize it.

Love is kisses in little parsonages, in tiny, crowded apartments surrounded by boxes, in a fixer-upper falling apart all around you, at the start of a brand new adventure, and you have absolutely no idea where you're going to live.

But it's ok because he'll still be with you to kiss you goodnight, wherever it is that you lay down your head.

Love is together.

There are many kinds of kisses in this world.

Love for me is kissing Kyle.

He was my first kiss, and he will be my last.

I love you, Kyle! Thank you for choosing me and going on this great adventure for Jesus with me!

I share this story for anyone who feels like love may never come your way. Don't be discouraged because you haven't met the "one" yet, or be disappointed or disillusioned if your romance doesn't read like the story you'd always had in mind. Just because love doesn't come to you in the precise package you had always envisioned doesn't mean it isn't real. Your Prince

Charming might not arrive in a horse-drawn carriage, holding a law degree, and carrying the keys to a house with a white, picket fence. He might come in a beat-up, red pick-up truck, wearing torn blue jeans, and holding the keys to a tiny parsonage in rural Arkansas with an unknown future in ministry. Mine did. And he is SO MUCH better than the dream I had for myself. When our spouse is sent from God, he or she will always come better than we imagined.

12

Put Down The Phone

I stood awkwardly leaning on my crutch and trying to find ways to make myself look less conspicuous. *It wasn't working.* Apparently crippled, pregnant women were not commonly spotted hanging out in the entryway of Walmart.

Looking back, maybe if had I started smiling and waving, people would think I was a greeter. Better yet, if I stood completely still, maybe people would think that I was a mannequin, perhaps simultaneously advertising maternity clothes and orthopedic aid!

"Can I help you?" another employee asked.

"Oh, I'm good!" I laughed confidently. A kind employee in an elf hat had already volunteered to fetch me an electric cart, but I doubted they even had one in stock. They rarely had one avaiable. Last week my husband had picked me up and tossed me into the back of a normal grocery cart along with our nearly two-year-old son. We got some great reactions from our fellow shoppers. This is "in sickness and in health" at its finest and most entertaining.

However, on this shopping trip, I was all by myself. The

prospect of crutching to the opposite end of the store was overwhelming. I had severely injured my knee near the end of my first trimester in a ridiculous accident involving sitting down in my car. This particular injury would normally have required immediate surgery. However, risks to the baby necessitated that I wait until after she was born to have it repaired.

In the meantime, I was working on ways to make my limp more attractive and socially acceptable. I was debating between peg-legged, pot-bellied pirate and retro dancer who moon-walked everywhere. It was more of an awkward sliding motion but if I waggled my hips maybe someone would think I was dancing. My husband had yet to approve of either of these two new identity choices.

I sighed with relief when I spotted my elf helper steadily making his way towards me in a coveted electric cart. I made sure to thank him profusely before climbing behind the wheel. After nearly running over two or three innocent bystanders I broke free into the produce section. Soon, however, I realized I was going to have greater issues than my poor driving skills.

The sounds the cart made indicated that it had not been maintenanced since, oh, *the foundation of Walmart.* The front right wheel squeaked and wobbled so loudly I feared it might fall off at any moment, and though I pushed the lever up to the highest speed, I went only about the pace of a turtle being pulled by a team of slugs. To top this off, the brake system was shot. When I tried to stop I lurched to a neck-snapping halt. The whiplash was accompanied by a sound similar to metallic nails grinding against a chalkboard.

I was determined, however, to get what I came for and gunned her for all she was worth. The next 20 minutes can be summarized in the following soundbite.

> *Squeak Squeak Squeak Squeak* **SCREEEEEECH**. *Ow! I am **SO** sorry, ma'am! My neck!! Is it possible to give an unborn baby whiplash?* **BEEP BEEP BEEP**. *Bang! Oh no... I'll just go the other way.* **SCREEEECCCCHHHHH**, *I sincerely apologize sir, I am not very good at this thing. Wow, I sure take up a ton of room, don't I? OW!!!! I think I'm going to have to see a chiropractor. Are they supposed to be laughing at me or with me? Don't mind me! Something is obviously wrong with my cart here. It's not me, really.* **SCREECHH!!! OW!!!**

I somehow managed to successfully collect my items. When I turned to begin the arduous journey back to the register, a crowd of sympathetic onlookers parted like the Red Sea. They were either being kind, or terrified of becoming roadkill. A red light began to flash on the cart's dashboard, indicating that my battery was about to die.

Fantastic. As I tried to imagine what I would do if the cart died right here in the middle of the store, I was hit with a sudden stroke of brilliance! This would make the BEST live Facebook video ever!! I could do a fake S.O.S. call pretending to be stranded in the middle of Walmart. I could include cute, clever phrases like, "Don't worry everyone! I landed close to Auntie Anne's pretzels, and the smell is reviving me." This was going to be GREAT!

"Nothing like drawing attention to yourself!" a well-meaning woman teased as she watched my agonizingly slow journey.

"Oh yeah!!!" I shouted back cheerfully, now eagerly antici-
pating my moment of awkward, supermarket glory.

Amazingly, I managed to make it to the front of the store
and through the checkout line before the inevitable happened.
Without warning, my cart to a stop, slammed nearly sending
me over the steering wheel. They should seriously consider
putting seatbelts on these things, maybe safety harnesses. My
stunt gathered the stunned attention of a bench of employees
on break.

"Don't worry!" a valiant young man popped to his feet," I
will push you to the front!"

"Hold on!" I held up a hand and whipped out my cellphone.
"I need to make a video!"

Traffic streamed around me as my brave, new friend poised
behind the chair, and I frantically fumbled to pull up Facebook.

WHAM! I was jerked to the side. A woman had somehow
gotten her cart wedged between me and the watercooler. As
she attempted to break herself free and my thumbs struggled
to launch me into internet stardom, my cart suddenly, miracu-
lously, launched forward. Maybe the impact had set something
straight in my geriatric ride.

"Never mind!" I called to my helper, secretly bemoaning the
loss of my golden moment. I decided I could at least salvage the
aftermath and held up my phone to record my violent ramble
through the exit. As I attempted to make this video as incredible
as possible, I noticed an older gentleman in a flannel jacket
staring me down. I ignored him and continued to try and come
up with witty and interesting things to say. I was busy doing
a terrible job parking my cart and being sad about my video
lacking the epic quality I hoped for when the older gentleman
who had been watching me so intently approached, breathing

heavily.

"Excuse me, could I have that cart?" He asked, in obvious physical distress.

"Of course!" I said, all thoughts of my lost moment vanished instantly as I noted his desperate expression. "I have to warn you, though, I think the battery is about to go dead."

"It's ok," he doubled over, hands clutching his knees, unable to catch his breath. "I have to have it. I have congestive heart failure."

I fumbled quickly to grab my bags so the poor man could have a seat. "I'll just sit here a while and let it charge." I nodded and gave some sort of awkward, saddened goodbye.

I felt sick as I hobbled my way back through the darkened parking lot. I had been so concerned with my moment of internet stardom that I had completely ignored this man who had been in obvious pain.

I wondered how often I had allowed my obsession with attracting social media attention to distract me from those around me who actually needed my love and my attention.

This is not just a personal struggle but a cultural epidemic. More than any other generation, ours is faced with the temptation to settle for *looking good rather than doing good.* Our culture values digital reputation above in-the-moment presence.

This social media-driven world has created a climate of self-absorption that has made it easy to confuse doing what is "tweetable," "likable," even "lovable" for doing what is loving, *what is right.* After a while, we start to equate what is "seen" and what is "noticeable" for what is life-changing and important.

God sees things differently. He says that when you do good, you are not even to let "your left hand know what your right hand is doing." (Matthew 6:3) He describes Himself as One who lives and sees in secret.

Jesus saved His strongest words of condemnation for those who performed their acts of righteousness in the streets for everyone to see and His promise of greatest reward for those who loved selflessly without regard for personal acclaim.

One day the lights will turn on. All of our hidden motives will be exposed and marched center stage. Our social media facades will be stripped away. We will stand naked and as we really are—deprived of the covering of our "likes" and our "shares" and our friends' lists. God will reward us not based on how much we were "liked," but on how much we loved.

Genuine acts of in-the-moment, face-to-face, love are the building blocks of Christ's kingdom. God broke the barriers of time and space to become *present* with us, to become Emmanuel. He demonstrated His love by closing the distance between us, putting on our flesh, and sharing life with us.

Christ became present with us so that we could learn how to be present with other people.

Let's be like Jesus. Let's give the present of our presence today. Put down your phone and look someone in the eye. Practice face -to-face, person-to-person love. We can't pour out our lives for people if we're not even looking at them or are too busy looking at ourselves.

This is the generation that wants to change the world. Let's start by loving the person right in front of us.

13

#TheGodList

"I found something you might want," my husband said, holding out his hand. The rainbow-striped, spiral notebook he offered me had seen better days.

He had found it lying on our oil-splattered garage floor. "Thanks," I replied, snatching it up eagerly. I have always been an obsessive journaler, and I consider the penciled-in pages of my previous journals my most prized possessions.

My love story with my husband is chronicled in texts and pictures, and Facebook posts. The only tangible record of my romance with Jesus is written here — scribbled lovingly in the crumpled, lined pages of my diaries.

I was especially excited to see this beat-up little book, even though I had no idea what it contained. I had been on the hunt for a particular journal entry from my college days. The entry concerned the nature of miracles and centered around the concept that real miracles are more about healed hearts than about healed bodies.

As I took the rescued journal from my husband, the worn pages flipped open automatically in my hands. My jaw dropped as my eyes took in the content — this was it. The notebook had opened to a journal entry about miracles from years ago.

I was stunned.

My husband later told me that he had originally found the notebook while cleaning out my parent's garage. He had come upon a cardboard box stuffed with old journals. Most of them had been destroyed by mold, but for some reason, he felt compelled to rescue just that one journal.

This was definitely going on my "God List." What's a God List?

For a few months, I had been keeping track of any moment in my life where I felt I had witnessed undeniable divine intervention. For lack of a better name, I called my growing archive "The God List." When I first started chronicling my list of miracles, I was primarily looking for larger, more "fantastic" events — money down to the exact penny at just the right time, protection from what could have been disastrous situations, unexplained physical healing —more of your "classic" miracle scenarios. While I experienced these sorts of supernatural occurrences, I found that the vast majority of my miracles were instances where God would show up and show me where I needed to be more like Jesus.

In a single day, I would hear a sermon, read a devotional, receive a text from a friend, and find an old journal article — all containing a nearly identical message. It was as if Heaven had a megaphone and was shouting, "Daughter, I can split the seas for you, reverse disease for you, pluck you from the fire, but what I really want to do, is to be formed in you. I want you to experience the wondrous purpose for which I made you—union with Me." C.S. Lewis once said:

The Christian story is precisely the story of one grand miracle, the Christian assertion being that what is beyond all space and time, which is uncreated, eternal, came into Nature, into human nature, descended into His own universe, and rose again, bringing Nature up with Him. It is precisely one great miracle...once you have accepted that, then you will see that all well-established Christian miracles are part of it. That they all either prepare for, or exhibit, or result from the Incarnation.[19]

In essence, any real, lasting miracle is simply a manifestation of the ultimate miracle — Christ's victory over death and the restoration of humanity's relationship with God. Our lives are meant to be little Gospel dramas, played out over and over for a watching world.

How do we become these living reenactments of the resurrection? How do we become living, breathing miracles? — We conform our lives to the pattern of the cross and pour ourselves out in love for other people.

God hammered this message deep into my heart when I noticed an old friend posting some concerning and frankly depressing statuses on social media. We'll call her "Sarah." Though we hadn't talked since we were children, I felt compelled to send her a "How are you?" message and invite her out to lunch.

We had a very encouraging meet-up and plotted some practical action steps to help Sarah break free of a difficult situation. I drove away marveling at the joy of witnessing the immediate transformation that overcomes a person when they realize they are seen, known, and not alone in this grueling earth journey.

A few days after my pow-wow with Sarah, I was puttering around our cluttered garage when the back of a photograph caught my attention. It was sticking up from a discarded box of jewelry and arrested my attention because I had been rifling through this same case the day before. Yesterday, the box was empty except for a tangled nest of pearls and rusty, silver bangles. How had this picture gotten in there? Where did it come from?

With the trembling sense that something incredible was about to happen, I plucked the photo from its hiding place and turned it over. One half of the picture was covered by a sticky note. The other was plastered with a smiling picture of myself as a teenager. I could tell my arms were wrapped around someone, but their face was hidden beneath the small, pink paper. On the note I had penned, "If his life was changed by one, 'How are you?' what does that mean for my life?"

I immediately recognized this as a reference from my favorite Christian-living book, "In The Footsteps of Jesus" by Bruce Marchiano.2 In this passage, the main character's life is forever changed when one of his professors takes the time to sit down and genuinely asks, "How are you?"[20]

As I pondered the significance of this quote, my fingers slid beneath the sticky note. Time seemed to slow as my trembling fingers peeled back the paper.

My heart stopped.

I stared down into Sarah's smiling face, my arms enfolded around her in a loving squeeze.

I was shocked. I had no memory of even seeing this girl since we were little children, and in this picture, we were almost adults. Though I later remembered the day this photo was taken, the odds that the only picture ever taken of us would be preserved and then mysteriously appear in my jewelry box 10 years later were, well... nearly impossible.

This was not a coincidence. This was God jumping up and down and waving His hands in my face.

"This is it!" He cried, "This is the miracle. This is the Gospel lived out — Me pouring my life into you so that you can pour My life into other people. As I chronicled in my growing "God List" shortly after this event:

> *It's all about loving people. The miracle is individual people seeing Jesus. He has set up a series of encounters for your life. That's why you're here so that through you, people can see Jesus. He Himself is the miracle this world needs. Feeling insignificant? God has a master plan for you to know Him and the privilege of showing Him. There is no more adrenaline-laced project in the world.*

One morning, shortly after this revelation, God deeply impressed a message on my heart. "For what does it profit a man to gain the whole world and forfeit his soul?" (Mark 8:36) We can seek every ecstatic experience this world has to offer, but it will equal a whole lot of nothing without Christ. Happiness and peace will continue to evade us.

As Rankin Wilbourne says, "It's curious because it seems as though we can do a lot of things apart from Jesus, and that most of the time we do. But Jesus is saying that apart from Him we can do anything but live." 4

I sensed that this message wasn't just for me. I had been praying for a particular friend named "Abigail" and invited her over to chat. Abigail had been chasing hard after happiness. She had joined every club, participated in every academic pursuit, pursued all the guys, and still found herself coming up inwardly empty. As we sat down on the porch swing, legs dangling in the sweet summer shade, she startled me when she remarked, "I've been thinking, and I realized that no matter what I do to try and find happiness, it won't work without God. He's what I need."

The same God who had spoken to my heart that morning had been speaking to Abigail as well, softening her soul to receive the life-giving message of grace. I was privileged to participate in a miracle that afternoon as I shared God's desire to become her one and only true source of joy.

From that point on, whenever the word "miracle" entered my mind, it came emblazoned with an image of sweet Abigail's face.

As time went on and my "God List" grew longer, I had the brilliant, maybe not so brilliant, idea to encourage others to join me in chronicling the hand of God in their lives. I posted a challenge on social media, inviting others to share their God stories using the hashtag, "#TheGodlist." I fantasized about crashing the Internet with stories proving that God's not dead and His work's not done. Can you imagine what would happen if all Christians everywhere shared their testimonies?

Everyone seemed to approve of the idea, and my video received several thousand shares. Unfortunately, though people were willing to share my post, almost no one actually shared their story. Instead, I received some nasty correspondence from atheists who made sure to let me know what a fool I was making of myself and how idiotic my efforts appeared to them.

What was worse, these attacks came from friends who had formally claimed to be Christians.

I had expected to receive at least some backlash but had not anticipated the assault to arise from people I knew and loved or the impact their remarks would have on me. My entire grand experiment felt like a failure.

I was discouraged and confused. Had God really been calling me to share my list? Had I just been imagining all these instances where I felt God was working?

After weeks of grappling with these tough questions, my discouragement reached a nearly unbearable crescendo. One morning as I drove shakily into my doctor's office, I pleaded tearfully to the Heavens, "God, if You're there. Give me a miracle. I'm begging You."

I didn't really know what to expect as I dried my face and attempted to look sane before entering the waiting room — a bolt of lightning? An audible voice booming from the ceiling?

As I reached the check-in counter and began fumbling around for my insurance card, a side door opened, and a discharged patient nearly walked into me.

I lifted my head, and there she was — Abigail.

My "miracle," standing there in the flesh.

I don't remember what we talked about, but I am sure I probably didn't make much sense.

The chances of meeting Abigail in the doctor's office that day were approximately zero. This wasn't like Mayberry, where you run into your pals on every street corner. I had to drive to a large city in a neighboring state to make the appointment. Abigail doesn't even live in my state!

I can confidently say that God sent me a "real" miracle that day. And it wasn't an audible voice from Heaven, a bolt of lightning, or spontaneous healing — *it was a person.*

If you're feeling dry and barren, discouraged by the broken-ness of our world, maybe you, like me, have been looking for

Him in all the wrong places.

Yes, God still heals, He still speaks, He still calms the storm. But the biggest, most impactful miracles we will experience this side of Heaven are human hearts made new by the grace of God.

As Ted Dekker said, "Whoever said a straightened hand was more dramatic than a healed heart anyway?"[21]

It certainly wasn't God. All the physical miracles Christ performed were wonderful but temporary. They all eventually reversed themselves.

The blind whom He made see would one day close their eyes in death.

The lame whom He made walk would one day lay down in a casket.

Lazarus was once again placed in a tomb, but this time, he didn't come out.

But the people who accepted Christ's forgiveness are even now experiencing the greatest miracle of all — *eternal life*.

Are you a recipient of this great miracle? — This mystery of Christ's death, burial, and resurrection that sets us free from our sin and enables us to began experiencing eternal life even now? "And this is eternal life, that they *know you*, the only true God, and Jesus Christ whom you have sent." (John 17:3, Emphasis Mine)

The only chance humans have to escape the ordinary, to find the kind of life we were made for, is in *knowing Jesus*.

Billy Graham, the great evangelist, lived what we all would consider an extraordinary life. He traveled the planet, be-friended celebrities, served as the personal confidant of many US Presidents, spoke on the most coveted platforms at the biggest stadiums in the world. When he was eighty years old, he had dinner with former Moody President, Joseph Stowell. Stowell began asking Graham about his life, wondering which of his exotic experiences had left the biggest impression. Graham surprised him when he said, "None of that...By far the greatest joy of my life has been my fellowship with Jesus. Hearing Him speak to me, having Him guide me, sensing His presence with me and His power through me. This has been the highest pleasure of my life!"[22]

As Christians, we get the best of the best. We get the excitement of pouring our lives out for other people. Even more than this, we get the adventure of *knowing the One who gave us life*.

If you have never experienced Christ's forgiving power, if you don't know Jesus, the cure is simple. It's as easy as recognizing your sinfulness and your need for Him, believing that He died in your place and rose again, and asking Him to forgive you and come into your life with His redeeming power.

"Jesus told them, "This is the only work God wants from you: Believe in the one he has sent." (John 6:29 NLT)

He's not offering you an easy life, a pain-free life, even a "successful" life.

He's offering You *Himself.*

When Christ takes up residence in our hearts, we don't just get to experience miracles. We get to *be* the miracle.

That's anything but ordinary.

Epilogue

"I'm afraid," she whispered.

He placed a comforting hand on her shivering shoulder and gave it a gentle squeeze.

"Of what?" He asked quietly, though He already knew the answer.

"Of what I can't see," she replied, gaze fixed dead ahead. From here, the future looked like a wall of cloud. It billowed up a yard from her planted feet. She blinked, hoping to clear the fog. "Of tomorrow."

"Can you see this?" He held up His hand an inch before her nose.

"Yesssss," she answered slowly, eyebrow cocked.

"Then take it," He whispered in her ear.

She didn't move.

He stepped before her and offered his hand again, palm up, reading for the taking.

She sighed and slid her fingers into His, but when He turned to go, she panicked.

"Wait!" she blurted.

He stopped and looked back, searching for an explanation.

"Where...where are we going?"

His eyes twinkled with some hidden treasure, one she was certain He would soon unearth.

"With Me," He answered simply, holding out His other hand.

She studied it for a moment, took in the creases, the calluses, the strength. His sleeves hung loosely about His wrists, revealing two matching scars — gruesome holes where flesh should have been.

She took the hand.

"Ready?" He asked.

"Yes," she replied, pulling herself into Him and resting her forehead on His chest. She gritted her teeth and braced herself.

Nothing happened.

He let out a loud chuckle.

"What?" she cried exasperated, throwing back her head, "What are You prolonging this for?!"

He released her hands and used His own to steady her face. With her chin up, their eyes locked in line, it was impossible to miss His reassuring wink.

"Perfect," He said. "Don't look away."

He reached down and took her lightly by the fingertips before taking a step forward. She followed hesitantly.

"What do you see?" He asked.

"Um..." she turned her head to look around, "I...."

With a gentle brush of the hand, He brought her back to face Him.

"Now...what do you see?" He asked again, slowly, deliberately.

She searched for something shockingly profound to say, but all she could come up with was, "You."

He grinned. "You Ready?"

"I guess."

They took another step. "What do you see?"

She sighed and began to search around when He righted her again. "No, what do you see?"

"I see...*You*."

"Perfect."

Her heart skipped a beat.

One more step.

"What do you see?"

This time she didn't even try to look away. She just kept staring up at her Shepherd.

Maybe she really was beginning to see.

"I see You."

"That a girl," He nodded and squeezed her hands.

One more step.

"What do you see?" He enquired a final time.

She tried to speak, but something was blocking her throat.

"You," she croaked softly.

He clutched her face in His hands. "That's all you ever need to know."

She smiled through her tears and whispered, "I'm ready for tomorrow now."

His eyes glinted with the Treasure that was Himself.

"Where are you going?" He asked innocently as if He didn't know the answer.

Really, He'd just been waiting forever to hear what she was about to say.

"I'm going with You, Jesus."

"Nevertheless, I am continually with you; you hold my right hand. You guide me with your counsel, and afterward you will receive me to glory. Whom have I in heaven but you? And there is nothing on earth that I desire besides you. My flesh and my heart may fail, but God is the strength of my heart and my portion forever." (Psalm 73:23-26)

Notes

THE INVERTED MOHAWK

1   Ludy, Leslie. "Reflecting His Radiance. " setapartgirl, 1 Oct. 2020, https://s
    etapartgirl.com/reflecting-his-radiance/. Accessed 2 May 2021.

HOT DOG. TRAIN. MIDNIGHT.

2   Goff, Bob. *Everybody Always: Becoming Love In A World Full Of Setbacks and
    Difficult People.* Thomas Nelson, 2018.

I LOST MY MONKS

3   Ortland, Dane. Gentle and Lowly: The Heart of Christ For Sinners. Crossway.
    2020.

4   Ortland. *Gentle and Lowly: The Heart of Christ For Sinners.*

5   Allen, Jenny. *Nothing To Prove: Why We Can Stop Trying So Hard.* Waterbrook,
    2017.

THE DAY I HUGGED JESUS

6   Tozer, A.W. *The Pursuit of God.* Christian Publications, 1948.

THE GREAT MORTARBOARD MALFUNCTION

7   Emory, Allan C. *A Turtle On A Fencepost: Little Lessons Of Large Importance.*
    World Wide Publishing Group, 1980.

8   Stowell, Joseph. *Simply Jesus: Experiencing The One Your Heart Longs For.*
    Multnomah, 2002.

9   Stowell, Joseph. *Simply Jesus: Experiencing The One Your Heart Longs For.*

10 Allen. *Nothing To Prove: Why We Can Stop Trying So Hard.*

GOD'S GPS

11 Wilbourne, Rankin J. *Union With Christ: The Way To Know and Enjoy God.*
    David C. Cook, 2016.

12 Nockels, Christy. *The Life You Long For: Learning To Live From a Heart of Rest.*
    Multnomah, 2021.

13 Nockels. *The Life You Long For: Learning To Live From a Heart of Rest.*

14 Nockels. *The Life You Long For: Learning To Live From a Heart of Rest.*

MY NOT SO CINDERELLA STORY

15 Smith, Judah. *Jesus Is: Find a New Way To Be Human.* Thomas Nelson, 2013.

16 Chambers, Oswald. *The Love of God: An Intimate Look At The Father Heart of God.* Our Daily Bread Publishing, 2015.

THE SNAKE-A-NATOR

17 Lucado, Max. *Just Like Jesus: A Heart Like His.* Thomas Nelson, 2012.

18 Tozer, AW. *Reclaiming Christianity: A Call To Authentic Faith.* Bethany House Publishers. 2009.

#THEGODLIST

19 Lewis, C.S. *The Grand Miracle: And Other Selected Essays On Theology and Ethics From God In The Docks.* Ballentine Books, 1986.

20 Marchiano, Bruce. *In The Footsteps Of Jesus: One Man's Journey Through The Life Of Christ.* Harvest House, 1997.

21 Dekker, Ted. *Blessed Child.* Thomas Nelson, 2006.

22 Stowell. *Simply Jesus: Experiencing the One Your Heart Longs For.*